# Fall Down Seven Times, Stand Up Eight

# Also By Kara L. Stewart
## Advanced Western Riding

# Fall Down Seven Times, Stand Up Eight

## Life Lessons for Everyday Warriors (e.g., the rest of us)

## Kara L. Stewart

Blue Imaginarium Press

First published in the United States by Blue Imaginarium Press,
an imprint of Blue Ascension Group.

Website
Scan to visit the
book's information page

# Dedication

If you've ever been pulled to explore something different than you've ever done before, drawn to move outside your comfort zone (even if it scares you a little… or a lot), or pushed into a situation you didn't ask for…

then you are an Everyday Warrior, and this book is for you.

Just remember.

You're stronger than you know and more capable than you think.

The secret is choosing to stand up, just one more time.      .

I'm rooting for you.

And I know you can do it.

# Contents

# Preface

"Fall Down Seven Times, Stand Up Eight" is a saying common in martial arts. It means getting back up after you've been knocked down. It means believing in yourself and not quitting. In the times of the Samurai, it meant fighting to the death, if that's what needed to happen.

When you first hear the phrase, you might think, "Yeah, right. I have no interest in fighting at all, much less to the death. And I have zero interest in being a martial artist."

Neither did I.

In fact, let's just say... I was the most unlikely martial arts student you could ever imagine.

When I started my journey in the Japanese martial art of Aikido, I was a 42-year-old woman. I'm short (a whopping 5'1" tall). I was carrying a few extra pounds around my hips.

Previous martial arts experience? Zilch.

Previous sports experience? None, unless you count one summer in 5th grade playing softball on our little mountain community's version of the Bad News Bears. We won one game.

Naturally athletic? Not so much. My sport of choice as a kid was riding my Arabian gelding, Surino, and entering local horse shows.

And the reason I got started in the martial art of Aikido in the first place? It certainly was not to learn to fight or even as a form of self-defense. It was to improve my horsemanship, of all things.

You've probably known people or you've heard stories about those lucky ones who have natural abilities. The natural athletes. The ones who pick up a complex physical movement in a few tries. The ones who excel in school even though they barely study. The ones who leap into the work world with swaggering confidence and, of course, their massive (and often very public) success soon follows.

Well, that isn't me. And that isn't this book, sharing stories of gifted people, dishing out advice and how-tos and stories of amazing accomplishments.

I don't know about you, but reading those books often has the opposite effect on me. Instead of feeling inspired and energized, I feel once again the deep niggle of "I'm not good enough and I'll never measure up" that has plagued me since childhood (despite being raised by incredibly supportive parents, who perhaps were the original Possibilitarians).

This book is about how a most unlikely student found her way into the martial art of Aikido and learned more than a few life lessons along the way. And while some of the lessons were learned in the dojo, others popped up in the most unusual places – the practice of life.

But this book isn't about me. This book is for the rest of us, the Everyday Warriors fighting the battles of daily life, and how we're all heroes of our own journey and those whose lives we touch.


I believe that these lessons are here for all of us. Practicing a martial art isn't required – there are plenty of places to practice in daily life. All that's required is that we come to life with a humble heart and the willingness to learn and be a beginner in the school – the dojo – of life.

I invite you to take the journey with me by filling out the questions at the end of each chapter. I can't wait to see where your path leads.

As we say in the dojo at the start of each class, "Onegaishimasu." Will you please practice with me?

# Acknowledgments

Standing on the shoulders of giants is a phrase that sums up how this book came to be. I've seen firsthand how it takes a village and special teachers to raise a horse-loving young girl into a horsewoman and a middle-aged woman and very unlikely Aikido student into a martial artist

Without so many dear and generous people, this journey would not have happened, and it certainly would not have turned out the way it has.

I'm sure I've missed the contributions of some people here, and for that I am truly sorry. If we have met somewhere along the path of life, rest assured you have been part of this story. I believe we all influence each other's journey and we are all connected.

So, thank you, to everyone who's been part of this adventure, for where it started, and where it's going. I can't wait to see what lies ahead.

**Mom and Dad**, for supporting and encouraging my dreams, love of horses, and love of words. Your love continues to guide and inspire me every day. What a gift to be your daughter.

**Mark Rashid**, for changing my life in profound ways. You didn't teach me horsemanship or introduce me to Aikido. You opened the door to becoming a better person. For your continued guidance, mentorship, and friendship, thank you.

**Crissi McDonald**, for being the light guiding me to what's possible with kindness, talent, and integrity. Physical size means nothing; heart and truth and authentic presence mean everything.

**Andrew Blevins Sensei**, for knowing how much more I am capable of and helping me discover what's possible with dedication, commitment, and the power of believing.

**Les Steveson**, for being my Sempai since my first day on the mat and teaching me through example what it means to be a martial artist and what happens when strength and encouragement converge.

**John Purvis**, for your strength and belief and practice over the years. We'll celebrate at Sunahama soon.

**Sempai and fellow students at Kiryu Aikido**: Cory Marsh, John Price, Charles Groff, Bob Lumley, Keith Gremban, Greg Johnson, Benjamin Sadorra, David Bell, Tyffany Price, Charles Bland, Katie Pham, Oleg Gorlach, Scott Blair, John and Johnny Purvis, and every student I've had the honor of practicing with and learning from along the way.

**Kei and Mariquita Izawa Sensei**, **Tim Sensei**, and **Tanshinjuku** dojo students, for your welcome into the Aikido family many years ago and setting the tone of the Aikido community. **Stephen Shaw**, for your Aiki spirit that carries on.

**Patricia Hendricks Sensei**, for being my role model as the strong martial artist I seek to become and for your compassionate, intuitive, heart-led leadership.

**Eva Murphy**, for your unshakable kindness and strength and friendship. Thank you for knowing how to save a life.

**Mary Mueller Rusin**, for your steadfast friendship, goodness, and support in countless ways that have helped more than I can ever say.

**Shannon Rae**, for being at Mark's clinic that day the tears threatened to drown life as I knew it, and in the weeks and months and years that followed. A Strongbow's waiting for us.

**Surino, Eddie, Serena**, for sharing your hearts and your wisdom and your grace with me. I'm a better human because of you.

**Essie Becker**, for always, always, always being there.

**Katie Reid**, **Suzi Zielinski**, and **Barbara Perzanowski**, for your friendship and wisdom and support in so many chapters of life.

**Jeannie Bruenning**, **Stephen Sisk-Provencio**, and **Dr. Carrie Johansson**, for being creative compatriots and readers, nurturing this idea into being.

**Charlie Puffer** and the Words and Music crew at Puffer's of Pismo, for encouraging the tender green shoots of emerging creativity.

The **Crisis Center in Castle Rock**, Colo., and **Ellen Sloan**, for helping me and so many reach a better place of safety and possibility.

**John**, for the adventures and growth and the ultimate gift: compassion. I wish you so much good.

**Laura Fraser**, for your wisdom and believing in a story that needed to be told. You changed everything.

**A Room of Her Own Foundation** and **Lighthouse Writers Workshop**, for helping voices be heard and stories be told around the campfire of community.

**Emily Rapp**, for shaping the mist of vision into a story with a beginning that led to so much more.

**Kelly Rae Roberts** and **Julia Cameron**, for shining the way to what can be if we just let go, believe, and trust the journey.

**Yosemite National Park**, for your strong, quiet presence that coaxed out the first mumbled words in the embrace of your silence.

# Foreword

Aikido is a martial art that has been known to transform people's lives in more ways than one. The discipline required to master this art is not only physical but also mental and spiritual. It is a journey that can take one from being a mere beginner to becoming a Deshi, a committed student, and eventually a teacher, passing on the knowledge and foundations of the art to others.

As a practitioner of Aikido for the past 37 years, I have had the privilege of experiencing both the role of the student and the teacher. Two decades ago, I founded Kiryu Aikido as a space to impart the invaluable lessons that I have learned along the way, and to serve as a solid foundation for those who are seeking to embark on their own journey. In 2006, fate brought Kara to the dojo, where she had the chance to observe a class. Little did she know, this encounter would mark the beginning of her own transformative journey, as she devoted herself wholeheartedly to the practice of Aikido.

Within the pages of this book lies a unique window into the incredible journey of Kara, a student of both Aikido and life itself. Through the teachings of Aikido, Kara has ascended the mountain of self-discovery and transformation, embodying the resounding message of perseverance inherent in the adage, "Fall down seven times, stand up eight." Drawing on the foundational teachings of this remarkable martial art, Kara's story is a testament to the profound impact that Aikido can have on one's life.

As her teacher and friend, I have witnessed her quiet and indomitable spirit face the challenges of Aikido head-on, mastering one of our secret techniques: the gateless gate. This technique involves showing up to class with a beginner's mind, and letting the rest take care of itself. Kara embodies this technique, and her unwavering dedication to Aikido has made her a rock in the dojo.

In this book, Kara shares her perspective on the journey of self-discovery and transformation through the eyes of a student. As a teacher, I have learned a lot from her insights, and I believe that this book will be a valuable resource for students of Aikido, teachers, and anyone who is ready to take that first step on their own journey, whether it's in Aikido or on another path.

A dojo is more than just a school; it is a place where the lessons of Aikido guide us on the way to discovering and facing our own challenges, both on and off the mat. This book is a testament to the power of those teachings, and how they can be nurtured by teachers and dojos to transform lives.

It has been a joy to read this book, and I am grateful to Kara for sharing a little bit of her soul and the lessons she has learned along the way. I hope that this book will inspire and guide others on their own journey of self-discovery and transformation through the teachings of Aikido and the insights she shared along the way.

Andrew Blevins, Kiryu Aikido Founder & Dojo Cho, 5th Dan Aikido

# 蒔かぬ種は生えぬ

*(Makanu tane wa haenu.)*

# Without sowing a seed, nothing will grow.

# 01 When the Student Is Ready...

My childhood passion was not athletics, and it certainly wasn't martial arts.

My passion was horses. Everything to do with horses. Smelling them, grooming them, taking care of them, loving them, petting them. One of my earliest memories was the sheer joy of riding the penny mechanical horse outside the King Soopers grocery store.

And the thing that made me nearly explode with excitement was going to the pony rides and having the chance to pet the silky mane, touch the soft nose, breathe the perfume of a real live pony. And then, oh my gosh! Getting hoisted up on this noble creature to experience riding! On a real pony! I was in heaven as this beautiful equine patiently carried me around in a circle under the tent.

Mom and Dad eventually saw that this passion for horses was not something that I was going to outgrow. We moved to the foothills west of Denver when I was six. They'd bought an old stone house that needed lots of work, and it came with a few acres and an old shed that could be converted into a barn. A barn meant there was a place for a horse! I was the luckiest girl in the world. (The photo here is of my beloved first horse, Surino, but we're getting a bit ahead of the story.)

A mile down the two-lane winding mountain road we lived on, a lady named Joanne Weber had horses. She was willing to trade riding lessons for me cleaning stalls. She taught me how to saddle her big Appaloosa mare, Trinka, and I had my first lesson. Up I went on this enormous gray horse, walking on a lunge line. I had no control of anything, but I was sitting on a real live horse. My love of all things equine was further cemented into my being.

Joanne believed in the old-world way of teaching a new rider to ride in balance by putting them on a lunge line. I later learned that the very talented riders of the famous white Lipizzaner stallions at the Spanish Riding School in Vienna spend six to eight months on a lunge line before being trusted to pick up the reins.

The lunge line is rope or flat webbing about 35 feet long, with a snap fastened to one end and a loop for a handle on the other end.

The snap end is fastened to the inside ring of the horse's halter, never the bit in a bridle. The horse moves in a circle around the trainer, who stands in the center of the circle.

With the trainer directing the horse in a circle, the rider could learn to sit in balance at the four-beat-walk, the two-beat trot, and the three-beat canter without needing to hold on with the reins. This meant the horse was spared from a new rider inadvertently pulling on the bit in the horse's mouth, causing confusion or pain.

After that first lesson with Trinka, Joanne put me on the lunge line many more times at the walk. It was weeks before she clucked to Trinka to encourage her to trot. It was like starting my lessons all over. The balance I'd gained at the four-beat walk now needed to keep me upright and connected softly to the saddle instead of bouncing up and down on poor Trinka's back. More weeks went by. Finally, I could sit the trot.

Next, Joanne clucked Trinka to pick up the canter, a three-beat gait that feels a bit like riding a rocking horse. Before I started taking lessons, I would have said that cantering and galloping were the same thing. Later I learned that, no, a true gallop is a four-beat gait, with each of the horse's feet hitting the ground in sequence at a different time. Race horses gallop; most other horses canter.

Learning to sit the canter was easier than the trot. It was like a wave, with Trinka's back rising with a moment of suspension when all four feet were in the air, then flowing downward as one hind foot landed first, then the diagonal pair of rear and front foot, and then the other front foot.

Later, I learned to feel which lead Trinka was on. During the canter, one of the horse's front legs will reach farther ahead than the other. If the left front leg reaches forward more, then the horse is on the left lead. If the right front leg reaches forward more, the horse is on the right lead.

Before the year was over, Joanne eventually allowed me to ride Trinka all by myself. Learning to use the reins to guide, not pull or punish, was the next layer Joanne helped me explore.

With a solid foundation of starting to learn to ride, combined with Joanne's teaching me horse care, grooming, feeding, and the ever-important skills of stall cleaning, in time, my parents agreed to bring home an assortment of ponies and horses that needed homes and that could teach me more about the fine art of horsekeeping.

There was Heidi the Shetland Pony, John the Quarter horse, Moses the retired Thoroughbred race horse, and a few others. Then, when I was seven, Mom and Dad brought Brandy home. My very first pony of my own.

Brandy was a pretty Welsh pony, dapple grey, with a blond mane and tail and a very strong opinion. She was young and barely trained when we got her. One of the rules of being a horseowner that I didn't know at age seven was that an unskilled human and an untrained horse don't always make for the best of partners. "Green" was the term used for untrained, and it applied to both Brandy and me.

One of my clearest memories of Brandy was when she pinned me in the corner of the corral and wouldn't let me out. I'm not sure if she was upset she hadn't gotten her evening ration of hay yet and thought that not letting me get past her to the feed room door was the solution, but there I was. Needless to say, I didn't ride Brandy much when the snow melted that spring. I was afraid of her.

The local horse-trader who'd sold my parents Brandy traded her for Flicka – the most gentlemanly, sweet black and white pinto pony. He gave me confidence, and it wasn't long before we were riding all over the place, often bareback, with just a halter. We joined the local 4-H club, the South Turkey Creek Equestrians, and began showing in our little local shows.

In a couple years, I outgrew my sweet pony Flicka and it was time to start looking for my first horse. Our neighbor Joanne had Arabians in addition to the huge Appaloosa Trinka. I loved their beauty and how smart they were. She set on the quest of finding a suitable Arabian for me, and within a few months, she found Surino.

Surino was 10 years old, tall at 15.2 hands (a "hand" is about is four inches), dark bay with dapple spots in his mahogany coat, and one white hind foot. He had the kindest eyes and a calm mind from his English Crabbet bloodlines. He had a quiet confidence and a wisdom. In no time, we spent nearly every waking hour together from elementary school through high school. One of my favorite daily events was sitting in his manger and reading to him as he quietly munched his hay. He didn't mind if I read a book of poetry for English class or reviewed the vocabulary from Spanish class. We were together, and that's all that mattered.

We started showing in the local 4-H club shows, and eventually in large Arabian shows in Colorado and Wyoming. Surino was my do-everything partner with the mind and willingness for any adventure. We showed in English riding classes with both hunt seat and saddle seat tack, plus western, halter, and showmanship. A few timed-event gymkhana classes now and then, like barrel racing and pole bending. We dressed up for costume class and channeled our inner cowboy in trail class, opening gates, dragging bags of trash, walking over bridges, and stepping over logs.

For us, showing was not about winning and ribbons. It was enjoying the connection we had, the complete trust in each other, reading each other's minds, transitioning between gaits with just a thought.

When I went to college, my parents took care of Surino during the school year until I came home in the summers. During my second year of college, advancing ringbone put a sad end to our riding. This progressive form of osteoarthritis in Surino's lower right front leg first showed up as occasional lameness during our rides. When it became more frequent, our vet x-rayed Surino. With the diagnosis of ringbone came the prognosis that our riding days were over.

Instead of riding, we went on walks together and enjoyed quiet time. By the time I graduated, the ringbone had progressed to the point where he was in pain daily. Another winter would mean even more pain. Surino had been my confidante and soul mate, and his presence had carried me through so many life phases. I couldn't imagine life without him. It was the hardest day when Surino and I finally said goodbye in September 1985.

Ironically, this month that included losing my dear friend Surino who'd been with me for so many years also included joining with a dear friend in marriage after meeting a couple years earlier in college.

John and I had been introduced by a mutual friend who thought we should meet because we'd both attended the same college in Colorado Springs. John had already graduated and I had two years to go. That one casual meeting with our friend at a dive bar with good Mexican food near the University of Denver led to dating over the summer and getting engaged the following spring during my senior year.

We were married September 28th. During the ceremony, the snow started falling. By the end of the reception at my parent's house near Conifer, a winter storm was building that would leave more than a foot of snow before it was finished.

After college and marriage, things like starting my career in communications, buying our first house, and all the parts of building a life meant I was horseless for 12 years. During this time, John and I moved from the western suburbs of Jefferson County to the rural town of Sedalia south of Denver, where we purchased five acres of horse property and a ramshackle house. There was room for a barn. And that meant a horse. Heaven.

It took another five years before I was ready to have a horse of my own again, but lucky for me, I met my neighbor Mary. She had horses, also loved Arabians, and invited me on trail rides.

It was wonderful. For the time being, I had horses in my life

again, even if they weren't mine. As we rode together, we developed a strong friendship. I liked Mary's strength, sensibility, humor, and deep compassion. We also shared a love of Basset Hounds.

One summer, a friend of Mary's read a book by a man named Mark Rashid. The title was "Considering the Horse: Tales of Problems Solved and Lessons Learned." It was a book of his experiences as a cowboy and head wrangler at a dude ranch in Estes Park. In his stories, often humorous, sometimes poignant, there was a lot about horse training without calling it training.

In fact, even though I'd been around horses most of my life and even at one time was on the path to be a professional horse trainer, the approach that Mark Rashid shared was different. He looked at horsemanship from the horse's point of view. And while Surino and I had developed a partnership so deep that our riding was a beautiful, effortless flow with imperceptible cues, based on complete trust in each other, I had to admit my teaching in horsemanship was from the old dominance mindset passed down by many traditional methods. Ideas like don't let the horse get away with things, be the boss, and never let the horse win were common tenets of those teachings.

On reading his book, I had a feeling that Mark Rashid was different. Very different.

Mary's friend found out how to contact Mark at the ranch in Estes Park. Before long, he was coming down to help a small group of us work with our horses in Mary's round pen set up in a corner of her pasture. Mark charged us mileage and I think we each gave him $20 or so per person.

I'll always remember the first lesson. I don't remember the issue we were working on – maybe it was helping a herd-bound horse learn to leave the safety of the group and be OK riding alone. Whatever it was, Mark's approach was fundamentally different. It wasn't about proving you were the boss, or forcing the horse to leave the herd, and certainly not about the "dangers" of letting the horse win.

It was about finding a different way through the issue – one that helped the horse stay calm and thoughtful, and actually learn to feel better about the situation, not be forced into submission because we humans had to win.

His approach was so soft, so quiet, so effective.

At that moment, I realized something. Even though I considered my riding and training to be quiet, when compared with Mark, I'd been shouting at my horses all these years. That dawning was as dramatic as a lightning bolt.

I knew this. If I ever had horses again, from now on I wanted to offer what Mark Rashid was offering. I wanted to discover a quieter way of working with them. And that was the key: Mark called what he did "working WITH horses." Not horse training, not being a trainer.

With that first meeting in the round pen and hearing Mark's quiet voice and calm direction as I worked with a little chestnut gelding in the late afternoon sun, I knew I'd found my teacher.

**Your Turn**: You may want to take a bit of time to answer the following questions. They may help you capture and explore your own thoughts as they relate to the concepts from this chapter of the journey.

Is there someone who intrigues you with their approach, especially with a task, hobby, or activity you've been doing a long time?

If you're a business manager, have you heard about a new way to inspire your team? If you're an artist, have you seen a new technique from an artist you want to try incorporating into your art? If you're a parent of young kids, is there someone who manages the beautiful daily chaos with grace and humor?

If an idea springs to mind, capture it here. What steps can you take to learn more about it?

If nothing springs up yet, don't worry. Your mind has been awakened to start noticing possibilities. Be patient and start noticing what bubbles up.

# 思い立ったが吉日

*(Omoitatta ga kichijitsu.)*

## It is a lucky day when you make up your mind.

# 02 Committing to the Path

For the next couple years, our little group kept inviting Mark down to Sedalia to work with our horses. I also enjoyed, and greatly appreciated, Mary's willingness to allow me to spend time with and ride her horses.

Eventually, though, the time was right for me to welcome a horse into my life again. Through kismet and the universe aligning, I met Eddie. But meeting Eddie almost didn't happen.

Eddie was a tall, athletic, bay Polish/Crabbet Arabian gelding. His registered name was Final Edition PR. The PR was from the Pine Ridge Arabians farm where he was born. The Final Edition part was because Eddie was the last of a special cross between his sire and dam, who died after Eddie was weaned.

When the search for my next special horse began, I knew I wanted an Arabian. I had found a young Shagya Arabian gelding named Solomon in Kansas. The Shagya bloodline produces Arabians that are noble, almost war-horse like. Stunningly beautiful, strong, substantial. The first time I saw a photo of the Shagya stallion Oman, my breath caught in my chest.

Solomon's owner and I had talked often, and she knew I was the right person for this nice young horse. When I said that I was very interested but couldn't afford what she was asking for him, she offered a price that I could manage.

Dad had eagerly agreed to fly us out to Kansas so I could meet the owner/breeder and ride Solomon. Everything was set. In just a couple weeks, I'd meet my new horse and make plans to bring him home.

Even though this was the plan, for some reason I'd agreed to go see an Arabian gelding for sale just a few miles away. From what the horse dealer described, he was quiet, sensible, and had been very successful in Hunter Pleasure class in Arabian shows. The only reason he was for sale was that the couple that owned him was divorcing and needed to sell their show horses.

On this bitter cold December day, I zipped up my coat and opened the front door to go see this local Arabian. To be honest, I wasn't all that interested, since I would soon be buying Solomon, but I kept the appointment anyway. The phone rang behind me. For some reason, I stepped back inside the house and answered it.

The breeder in Kansas was calling, and her voice was sad. She so wanted to sell Solomon to me, but she'd had a full-price offer from another buyer. The difference was several thousand dollars. As much as she hated to say it, she wouldn't be able to sell him to me.

Huh. I was shocked and disappointed, and thankful she let me know. My appointment to see the other horse was in 30 minutes. I headed to the barn with a clean slate and an open mind.

Eddie was standing tacked up with an English saddle and snaffle bridle in the middle of the large indoor arena. His soft breath formed steam curls that rose in the frigid air. His face had the slightly dished profile from his Polish/Crabbet bloodlines, not the pronounced dish of the Arabians with Egyptian bloodlines commonly chosen for portraits or sculpture.

Ken, his owner, was a kind man. I could tell how much he cared for Eddie by the way he gently handed me the reins.

"This is Eddie," he said. "I don't want to sell him but my ex-wife said she'd fight me in court and insisted that neither of us could keep him." He looked like he might cry as he stroked Eddie's long, velvety winter coat.

"Hello, Eddie," I said softly. He turned his face toward me and lowered his head just a bit. I put my hand on his shoulder and stood for a minute. His breathing was slow, his eyes soft.

We took a slow walk together around half of the arena, then came up to the mounting block. I checked the girth and let down the stirrups on the hunt seat saddle he was wearing. He stood quietly as I adjusted the length on both sides, and didn't move as I stepped onto the mounting block and settled gently in the saddle.

We walked a few laps of the arena to warm up, then picked up a trot for a few strides. Back to the walk for another lap. It was so cold and I didn't want him to get sweaty. We trotted again and picked up a canter. In just a few strides, we came back to the walk and took another lap around the arena before coming back to the center.

I dismounted and stroked Eddie's neck, then felt between his front legs. He was warm, but not sweating.

"I like Eddie a lot," I said to Ken.

"And I like how quiet you are with him," he said. "My ex-wife was, uh, uptight… winning was really important to her."

He added, "I think Eddie deserves better, and I think you'd get along really well."

With that, Eddie came into my life. On Super Bowl Sunday, January 25, 1998, on the same day the Denver Broncos won their first Superbowl, Eddie was delivered to Sedalia and our life together began.

And an interesting thing happened as that long winter turned to spring and Eddie and I started riding more frequently.

Based on the bond and relationship I'd had with Surino, I assumed that I'd pick right up from there with Eddie. Eddie, however, had other ideas, and I soon learned the first lesson of many that Eddie would teach me. He was Eddie. He wasn't Surino with a different name, a smudge of white on his brown forehead, and three white socks. And I needed to honor him and the special horse he was, not a replacement for Surino.

I soon learned I needed to clear my slate and empty my cup, and I turned to Mark for help.

Eddie and I attended many lessons with Mark, including week-long clinics out of town. The learning during these was exponential. Because I wanted more people to experience Mark's teaching, I started hosting clinics so others could benefit from his approach.

Over time and with Mark's help, Eddie and I developed that soul connection and unwavering trust that brought our partnership to a new level. For example, in one clinic I asked about exploring walk/canter transitions. When riding horses, the typical way of transitioning up to the faster gaits was to start at the walk, ask the horse to speed up a bit and start trotting, then speed up a little more until they are cantering.

Going from a walk directly to a canter was an advanced movement that needed strength and agility from the horse and a connection between horse and rider that made clear what was desired. By skipping the trotting steps in between, the horse needed to generate power in his hindquarters to push off into the canter instead of letting the faster pace of the trot pull him into the canter.

Mark countered. "How about a halt/canter transition?"

I looked at him. Really? I didn't actually ask this question, but it was swirling above my head.

At least with the walk/canter transition I was asking for, Eddie and I would have a little forward momentum. We'd skip the trotting steps, but we would be moving.

With Mark's suggestion of a halt/canter transition, there would be no gradual increase in speed. We'd be standing still, then leap into a canter at the first movement of Eddie's body. It would be like a runner in the starting blocks, going from motionless to sprinting in a second, with no steps in between.

I knew that if Mark had suggested this option, he believed it was possible. As our teacher, he knew we were capable of more than my limited view of what I thought we could do.

We headed out to rail of the arena. With Mark's voice guiding us, we focused on connecting our energy. I could feel the internal spring of energy in Eddie's body coiling and releasing. We started with walk/canter transitions. They were soft, connected. Beautiful.

Then, using that same connection, with only my exhale as the cue, Eddie and I were soon making halt/canter transitions – something I never thought possible.

For good measure, Mark also guided us into trying flying lead changes using breath. With these, my exhale was the cue for Eddie to change his lead at the canter in mid-air.

My smile could have lit up the world beyond that arena with joy at the partnership with my dear Eddie. And this was just the start of the things Eddie and I could do as trusted partners.

During these years I was learning from Mark, he had started practicing the martial art of Aikido. He was finding many benefits and parallels to his approach of working with horses – blending, redirecting energy, using breath, balance, center, the power of softness – and he invited students to explore it if they had any interest.

That was about all he said; it wasn't an instruction to start Aikido, just a passing comment.

For whatever reason, I was intrigued. Martial arts had never interested me, but I started looking for a school (called a dojo) near where I lived.

There were a few Aikido dojos in the Denver area, but I ruled out several, including the largest school in Colorado, because it was a 45-minute drive and I knew I needed to have a closer dojo so that the drive wouldn't affect my commitment to attend class.

One Aikido dojo, Kiryu Aikido, was located about 15 minutes from me. It sounded good, so I sent an email to the address on their website asking about classes, times, whether they accepted complete beginners, etc. The Sensei, Andrew Blevins, wrote back with details. I thanked him and let him know that I had some business travel coming up and once it was out of the way, I'd begin training.

He later told me that this is what 98% of potential students say – they'll start practice when they can fit it into their schedule, and they never do….

But I meant it.

In between my business trips, I asked Blevins Sensei if I could come watch a class. He said of course, and mentioned that they had a six-week beginner's class. Not a separate class, but integrating new students into practice at a slower pace, which he'd found to be much more effective in helping students learn and improve.

I shared all of this with John, as well as the horsemanship connection that Mark was experiencing with Aikido. John had taken some Tai Kwon Do as a kid and was interested in seeing what Aikido was about, so one cold winter night in January 2006, we drove to the dojo.

Kiryu Aikido practiced in a gymnastics studio. The space was huge, with a blue spring floor as the focal point of the big metal building. On the far wall was the vault jump runway. Several sets of uneven bars and balance beams filled another space. Near the entrance door was a trampoline and deep pit filled with foam blocks.

After Blevins Sensei welcomed us to the dojo, John and I took a seat on the metal bleachers to watch class. Every student wore a white jacket as part of their practice uniform. Some wore white pants, while others wore blue or black wide-leg pants that looked a bit like culottes and had an intricate bow tied around the waist to hold them up. Students with the white pants had a belt tied around their jacket. Most belts were white, a few others were yellow, green, or brown.

We watched as they first did warm ups: stretching their wrists in odd ways, falling down at different angles, slapping the mat with their hand, and then getting back up like nothing had happened. Then they formed a single line and began to do front rolls around the perimeter of the large blue mat. These were very different from the rolls I remembered from my non-illustrious attempts at gymnastics as a kid.

Then the students kneeled down in a line. Sensei demonstrated a movement with one of the students. When it was done, students paired up, first bowing to each other and saying some long word in Japanese, and taking turns practicing the movement. One student did it four times, then they switched.

This went on for several minutes. Then Sensei said a shorter Japanese word and the students lined up again, kneeling as they watched the next demonstration.

After a few movements, Sensei came over and asked if we had any questions. It was all so foreign; I couldn't think of anything to ask. We thanked him for letting us watch a class and I shared that I was looking forward to starting practice.

On the way home, I asked John if he was interested in taking the beginner's class. "Naaa," he said, "it's not my thing. But you do it and have fun."

In the weeks leading up to my first class, I shared with Mark that I'd found a dojo. He was excited for me, and then gave me one piece of advice: commit to practice for a year.

Aikido, he said, was a complex art. By giving it a year, I would know if I wanted to integrate it into my life. Not giving it a year wouldn't be a fair assessment. Trusting Mark as my teacher, I took his advice to heart.

If I was going to do this, I would commit to a year.

**Your Turn**: You may want to take a bit of time to answer the following questions. They may help you capture and explore your own thoughts as they relate to the concepts from this chapter of the journey.

Is there project or a practice you want to begin? Is there something that's been calling you, or that you're curious about? Don't worry if you're not "good at it." The practice is the goal, not the accomplishment.

What's a reasonable amount of time you can commit to doing it? While it may not be a year, giving any new endeavor a fair amount of time can get you through the scary, messy, awkward, "I'll never be any good at this" stage and into the first stages of understanding.

By then, you'll likely know if it's something you want to commit to.

# 物は試し

*(Mono wa tameshi.)*

## Things have to be attempted (so don't give up at the beginning).

# 03 Becoming Comfortable with Discomfort

With my business travel wrapped up, it was time to start practice! As the day of my first practice got closer, my emotions were all over the place.

Was I nervous? Check.

Scared? Check.

Excited? Check.

Worried I would hold the other students back? Check.

Looking forward to trying something so new to me? Check.

Afraid I wouldn't be able to do it? Check.

Dreading the possibility that the other students wouldn't welcome me, like the new kid in the cafeteria that no one wants to sit with, much less invite to sit with their group? Check.

When I dug deeper, this fear – still lingering from my childhood as a quiet, introverted kid – was the biggest. Check, check, and triple check.

With the demons of not fitting in shouting loudly, I'm not sure how I plucked up enough courage to pull on a pair of purple sweat pants and a long-sleeved white t-shirt on a cold Friday night. It was February 3, 2006.

I drove to the dojo and pulled open the heavy metal door. Walking alone down the hallway to the practice space, with throbbing fluorescent lights, I felt a bit like Rocky walking to the ring. Ok, maybe that's a bit of an exaggeration, but while I still felt fear, I also noticed a strange, yet quiet, sense of

exhilaration… and maybe a little pride that I was doing something so very different for quiet, little me.

The class flowed just like the one I'd watched with John a few weeks before. Sensei showed a technique, we got a partner, bowed, said an unintelligible Japanese word (which I mumbled). Then we took turns practicing it four times each. New technique, new partner.

The biggest difference was that I, thankfully, wasn't expected to do the rolls the rest of the students were doing. What a relief.

Instead, one of the students wearing the blue pants took me to the side of the mat, where he showed me how to keep a big, strong circle with my arms, kneel on the mat, and then roll gently over one shoulder. I gave it a try.

My roll? Completely square, with sharp edges, not the flowing circles like his.

What I noticed most, however, was how incredibly dizzy I was after just a couple attempts. The room was spinning and I had to pause a second for it to stop. I wondered if my long history of inner ear issues and infections as a kid was causing this, and if I'd ever get over it.

Oh boy, I thought. This could be a very long, very dizzy year.

And what about my worry of not being included in the cool kid's clique of students – all of whom looked so confident, so smooth, so competent? It disappeared at the start of the first technique. With each technique that Sensei demonstrated, a new student came over to work with me. They didn't get upset that I knew nothing, was clumsy, slow, and out of shape. They were just helpful and kind. Imagine that.

Because Aikido is reciprocal, you're either throwing or you're being thrown in every technique. Later I learned that Nage is the person doing the technique, Uke is the person receiving the technique (and usually being thrown or pinned), and "ukemi" is the word for learning how to fall and protect yourself from incoming energy. But unlike some other martial arts, where energy may be met with force or blocking the movement, Aikido is about going with the movement, absorbing it with your body, redirecting it, and letting it dissipate.

Sounds elegant and easy, right? Maybe for a toddler learning to walk, or someone with a long history as a gymnast. The rest of us enter adulthood with a lot of years practicing being rigid, avoiding falling at all costs, and viewing being thrown as losing the fight.

But in Aikido, being thrown is not losing. It's part of learning both sides of a technique – one is not possible without the other. Like light needs dark to exist, and vice versa.

In the warm-ups, I could see we were practicing how to fall in a controlled way. We practiced keeping our arms tucked in and not reaching out with a hand to break our fall. When it came time to make a partner and practice the technique, now I was understanding the reason for these movements in real time and for a real reason.

But even falling to the mat in slow motion, as Sensei instructed me to do as a new student, was a bit painful. And completely foreign.

I also realized that while falling was not comfortable and hurt a bit, I wasn't injured. And the pain went away very quickly.

As I kept doing it, however, I realized some things. First, this whole falling thing was brand new. I mean, really. What normal, rational adult makes the choice to fall, get up, fall, get up, and keep doing it for an hour?

I started to notice my partner's falls and glanced around at the other students. The only word I could come up with to describe their falls was "elegant," and it sure didn't look like they were in pain with each fall. Maybe there was a way to get to that side. Maybe the pain would go away with more practice falling.

As I tucked my leg and lowered myself to the mat again, I could see that learning to trust the fall – knowing that my body would learn to take care of itself – might be the biggest reward of this whole journey.

After class, I quietly asked Sensei what the word was that we used when bowing and what it meant.

"The word is Onegaishimasu, and you pronounce it Oh Nay Guy She Moss. Essentially it means 'please practice with me.' The full meaning is deeper, but that's the jist of it," he said.

He added, "Then, at the end of a technique and the end of class, we say Doumo Arigatou Gozaimasu – it sounds like Dough Moe Are Ee Gato – which means 'thank you very much.'"

"Ah, thank you," I said. I made a mental note of my first two Japanese vocabulary words.

**Your Turn**: You may want to take a bit of time to answer the following questions. They may help you capture and explore your own thoughts as they relate to the concepts from this chapter of the journey.

Have you experienced something that causes discomfort because you're new to it? Whether it's physical or mental, has the discomfort made you want to say "I don't want to do this"?

Our ego doesn't like feeling not in control, and our brain tries to protect us from getting hurt. But when we stay with that discomfort and trust that it's just a phase of learning, we can learn to become comfortable with discomfort. The next time you're doing something new, what's a phrase you can tell yourself to stay with it and see what happens?

# 八十の手習い

*(Hachiju no tenarai.)*

One may study calligraphy at 80. (It's never too late to start.)

# 04 Beginner's Mind, Part I

Driving home from my first class, my head was spinning – both from the dizziness of rolling and the wonder of what on earth I'd just experienced. The techniques, the strange words, the foreign feeling of moving my body in multiple planes. Falling, getting up, bowing.

Everything about that class was foreign to me.

Everything about that class was challenging, both physically and mentally.

Every part of my body had a valid reason to say, "Yeah, no. I tried it. Aikido isn't for me."

Yet for some reason I will never understand, Aikido whispered to me and asked, "Would you like to join me?" And I whispered back, "Yes."

A resounding Yes.

And so began my path as a most unlikely student of Aikido.

As I bowed into my second class, I noticed something very different about the learning. For as long as I can remember, I've been blessed (or plagued… depends on the day) with a deep "good student" mindset. This means I study very hard, take it very seriously, and try to get an A on every test. I love learning, but I also have to work hard for my learning and have the inner need to try my best.

In fact, once I took Biology 100 in college as a pass/fail option. Even then, I couldn't dial down the studying to merely pass the class. I put in as much effort as if I was working toward an A.

For me, it's always been all or nothing, and that might be because I have a hard time learning certain things. They don't stick.

I was never the kid in high school or college that barely studied and still got good grades. I studied diligently because that's the only way I could learn. Later in life, when more was known about different

learning disabilities, I wonder if I have one. All I know is my brain doesn't seem to work as quickly as some people's do. And certainly the brain-to-spoken-word connection seems slower in me.

Yet from my first class in Aikido, for some reason my "good student" mindset didn't kick in. In fact, just the opposite happened. As I was trying to replicate the movement that Sensei showed, refreshing and novel thoughts like these lit up my brain:

I am a beginner!

I can't be good at Aikido because I just started!

I can't know all the answers!

I can come to class and just learn!

I can focus on doing my best and not get frustrated that I learn slowly!

I can gratefully accept the teaching I'm being offered!

I didn't know anything about the idea of the Beginner's Mind or the Zen parable of the empty cup at the time, but that's exactly what I was doing and how I was approaching being an Aikido student.

The Beginner's Mind concept from Zen Buddhism meant keeping an attitude of eagerness, openness, and lack of preconceptions during any form of learning, no matter how much you already knew about the subject. It was having an inquisitive mind ready to learn and see the topic with fresh eyes – just like a brand-new student and beginner would do. The challenge was keeping this mindset even as you continued to learn and add layers of understanding.

In the empty cup parable, an eager student arrives at a teacher's house to learn. The student has read and studied and practiced much before arriving, and is excited to add more knowledge and depth under the tutelage of the respected teacher. However, the student is turned away day after day after day.

Finally, one day, the teacher invites the student in and they sit at the table. The teacher begins to pour a cup of tea for the new student. When the tea reaches the top of the cup, the teacher keeps pouring. It overflows, and still he keeps pouring.

"Stop! The cup is full!" the student exclaims.

"Exactly," says the teacher. "You are like this cup. You are full of ideas. You come and ask for teaching, but your cup is full; I can't put anything in. Before I can teach you, you'll have to empty your cup."

I could not control the speed at which I was learning. The only thing I could control was coming to every class, paying attention, and doing my best. The learning, how long it took, how "good" I was, and all the rest would take care of itself.

So every class, I took more awkward falls. I attempted more square rolls and waited for the room to stop spinning. I mumbled foreign words. I bumbled my way through the movements.

Seeing Sensei demonstrate a technique and then trying to make my body do something similar was a continual source of learning. I'd see him demonstrate, clear as day. Put your left arm out and your partner grabs your left wrist. Drop your elbow and pivot around it. Bring both hands up like you're lifting a big rock above your head. Turn your center to give the rock to your partner. Allow your hands to continue the arc and float down to your waist area. End with your palms up like you're holding a tray.

So easy.

And then I'd try it. The translation from my eyes to brain to body would short-circuit. I might get the pivot but not lifting the rock, or using only one hand to lift the rock. Or I'd pivot the wrong direction. Or any number of interesting variations as my body tried to translate seen motion into felt movement.

And I'd try again.

Class after class at the dojo, the freedom of being a beginner just encouraged me to try again. And over time, the very basic movements started dialing into my muscle memory.

---

**Your Turn**: You may want to take a bit of time to answer the following questions. They may help you capture and explore your own thoughts as they relate to the concepts from this chapter of the journey.

When you start a new activity, how do you normally approach it? Do you have a Beginner's Mind? Do you expect yourself to be good at it from the start?

What can you do to foster a Beginner's Mind in an activity you try?

Can you imagine bringing a Beginner's Mind to the activities you enjoy already? What do you think the benefits of that might be?

Have you experienced the Beginner's Mind in an activity? What did that feel like?

# 涓滴岩を穿つ

*(Kentekiiwa o ugatsu.)*

# Drops of water will bore through a stone.

# 05 Dedication

In my faltering, one-awkward-step-at-a-time method of learning, six weeks went by. I'd completed the beginner's program!

When I started practice on that cold February night, I'd made myself a little promise. Actually, I made two promises. The first promise was that I'd commit to practice for a year. For the last six weeks, I'd built my schedule around dojo practice. It wasn't hard to do; it's just what I did on those certain days of the week.

Now, six weeks later, I could see the progress I'd made. I still couldn't do a round front roll very well. Translating a technique from seeing it to doing it was still a challenge. But some of the basic movements we did every class were starting to make a little more sense. Or, rather, I was able to link together a few movements and not be completely lost.

I could also tell I was getting in better shape. And the falls we did in every technique? They weren't hurting as much. All this was after just six weeks.

The second promise was that I'd celebrate my first milestone of six weeks of practice by buying a gi – my first-ever martial arts uniform – and my first set of Aikido weapons.

I went to the small martial arts supply store on Federal Boulevard in the western suburbs of Denver. A woman owned the store, and she outfitted me in the white jacket and white pants of the keiko gi. Sensei suggested I get the heavier weave judo gi to add a little padding for front rolls and ukemi.

She held up the jacket and showed me how it closed with the left side overlapping the right. The reverse, she said, meant you were at a funeral. I wasn't sure if she meant at your own funeral or at someone else's.

As I held up the pants and took a look at them, all I saw was a long, white rectangle. Not form fitting in any way, no zipper, no real structure. They had double fabric on the inside of the pants over the knees. I didn't yet know that knee-walking, called "shikkou," was a thing, much less Suwari Waza (techniques from kneeling) and Hanmi Handachi (techniques where you're kneeling and your partner is standing). The pants also had a gusseted crotch for more freedom of movement.

With no zipper or buttons, the pants closed with a long drawstring that cinched up the fabric around my waist. Once I pulled them on and stepped out of the dressing room, the lady cinched them up a little tighter. I looked, I thought, like a white sandwich bag tied with a twist tie.

My new gi also came with a white belt. My first white belt! The only problem? I had no idea how to tie it properly.

The next class, I didn't walk straight to the mat in my purple sweats like I had for the past six weeks. I took a detour to the ladies restroom and put on my stiff new gi for my very first practice in uniform.

Standing at the edge of the mat, I held my jacket closed over my white t-shirt. With patience and humor, my Sempai John-san showed me how to tie my white belt in the proper way.

Sensei reminded me to practice tying my belt several times a day until it became muscle memory.

With that, I bowed onto the mat and lined up in seiza in my place at the end of the line as the lowest ranking student. I wasn't actually even yet at the first white belt rank of Rokkyu, the sixth degree of the lower level Kyu ranks. But I was here, in my dazzling white, stiff new gi, ready for the next steps of the journey.

**Your Turn**: You may want to take a bit of time to answer the following questions. They may help you capture and explore your own thoughts as they relate to the concepts from this chapter of the journey.

What steps can you use to dedicate consistent time to your practice? How can you build it into your life?

What's a mini reward you can give yourself for accomplishing your first milestone?

# 必要は発明の母

*(Hitsuyou wa hatsumei no haha.)*

# Necessity is the mother of invention.

# 06 Asking for (and Accepting) Guidance

A couple months after I started my practice at Kiryu Aikido, Sensei shared with all of us students that the dojo would be moving to a new location – the Littleton YMCA. It was just a few minutes away and we'd have access to the amenities of the facilities, like showers and locker room.

Because the room we would be practicing in didn't have mats, Sensei would be ordering 32 thick martial arts mats. We'd carry the mats into the room at the start of practice and take them out at the end of practice.

As I listened to this news, I realized my time on the cushy spring mat of the gymnastics studio was ending soon. I knew the mats would be much more firm, and I knew my ukemi needed to be better – my rolls needed to be more round and my falls more secure and consistent.

After class that night, I shared with Sensei that I wanted to improve my rolls and falls before we left the comfort of the spring mat. Would he consider doing an extra ukemi class? He was happy to do so.

The next week after our regular class, everyone was welcome to stay for an extra hour of ukemi practice.

Most students stayed and we started in to our extra practice. We did side falls and back falls. Each time, we slapped the mat with our bottom arm at a 45-degree angle, making sure our feet were in the right position. We tucked our chin.

And we did rolls. Over and over, we rolled. My rolls got a bit rounder as the practice went on, and the square edges of my body slowly became a bit more circular. Notice I said "a bit" rounder and more circular. I had a long way to go before my rolls were actually round and strongly fluid like Sensei's and the other students.

As we lined up on the edge of the mat to do another round of front rolls, my Sempai Les-san caught my eye. He smiled and gave me a double thumbs-up. Then he mouthed the words, "Awesome! Now just 1,000 more!"

I smiled back, surprised and appreciative of his silent comment and encouragement.

My rolls were not awesome. But I could feel they were better than when we started the extra practice. And he knew I was trying and that's what mattered. I was doing my best to incorporate the teaching of Sensei and try again. And again.

At the end of the class, I had the confidence that I could take rolls on the new mats in our new dojo home. And I knew they'd only keep getting better the more I practiced.

Nowhere to go but up, I thought.

**Your Turn**: You may want to take a bit of time to answer the following questions. They may help you capture and explore your own thoughts as they relate to the concepts from this chapter of the journey.

What is something you'd like to improve that, right now, isn't as good as you'd like it to be?

What will help you improve? More time to practice or getting some additional instruction?

Who can you ask for help with getting better?

# 叩けよさらば
開かれん

*(Tatake yo saraba
hirakaren.)*

# If you knock, the way will
be opened.

# 07 A New Perspective

About six months after I started training, Sensei shared with us that there was an Aikido seminar coming up in the Boulder area. It was hosted by Kei and Mariquita Senseis' dojo Aikikai Tanshinjuku, and their good friend and colleague Yasumasa Itoh Sensei from Boston would be the guest instructor.

After class, I asked if it would be appropriate for me to attend. Being such a beginner, I wasn't sure if it would be way over my head or if it was meant only for higher-ranking students.

"You've got enough of the basic movements and an understanding of the names," he said. "For where you are now in your training, I think it would be a good experience for you."

With that vote of confidence, I signed up for my first Aikido seminar. As the date got closer, I noticed I had many of the same questions/fears as I did when I was about to start practice at Kiryu Aikido.

Could I do it? Would I hold others back? Would I be welcomed?

I was excited. And I was very scared at the same time.

The morning of the seminar, I found my way to the women's locker room and started changing into my gi.

A woman next to me was doing the same. As she pulled her black belt out of her bag, she introduced herself.

"Hi, I'm Mariquita," she said, with a smile and a slight nod.

My brain quickly connected the dots. This was Mariquita Sensei, co-host of the seminar and co-owner of Tanshinjuku dojo.

"Hello Mariquita Sensei," I said and bowed. "It's so nice to meet you!"

She asked how long I'd been training, and we chatted about what I thought of Aikido so far.

"It's really challenging for me," I said, "but I love it. I'm not sure why."

As I finished tying my white belt, she said something that stayed with me forever and has shaped my practice ever since.

"Today, don't think that just because you're a new student you have to practice only with the white belts," she explained. "Do your best to practice with higher-ranking students and the black belts. You're here to learn, just like they are, and working with higher-level students will help you learn more."

"Hai," I said. "Thank you for sharing that with me. I look forward to practicing with you."

Mariquita Sensei's advice echoed the approach in our dojo. Sensei said that our job as students was to work with everyone. Another point he'd shared was that when an Uke had been used to demonstrate a technique, the rest of us students needed to quickly say "Onegaishimasu!" and bow to the Uke to practice with them. It was both etiquette – not to leave Uke stranded and waiting for a partner while all the other students paired up – and it was our opportunity to practice with the person who'd just experienced the technique firsthand from the Sensei.

The seminar was a great experience. I worked with everyone I could. Some of the big, flowing techniques of Itoh Sensei's style were beyond my comprehension, but it didn't matter. We were all there to learn together.

We may have started as strangers from many different dojos in the morning, but by the afternoon, we'd become friends sharing the path of Aikido.

**Your Turn**: You may want to take a bit of time to answer the following questions. They may help you capture and explore your own thoughts as they relate to the concepts from this chapter of the journey.

Are you thinking of taking the risk and challenging yourself to take a next step? Some examples might be signing up for your first 5K race, entering a competition, submitting work for a juried writing class or art exhibit. When you think about it, how do you feel? Excited? Scared? Both?

Have you had an experience where someone you admired gave you advice that changed the course of your training or your life? What was the advice? How did it affect you?

忍の一字は
衆妙の門
*(Nin no ichiji wa juumyou no mon.)*

# Patience/endurance is the gate to success.

# 08 Be Kind... For Everyone's Fighting a Dragon

When I started practice that first night at Vertical Sports, I met the only other woman in our dojo.

Linda-san was a brown belt – the level below black belt – and I was in awe. I honored her accomplishment and the dedication she'd put in to earn it. Achieving that rank was something I aspired to… someday. But that day was a long, long time in the future and I didn't think about it as a mountain to summit. I just did what I could do – show up to class and practice hard.

From my perception, Linda-san was coming along quickly in her practice. When I was her partner, she seemed to pick up the technique quickly. I liked that she was strong and sturdy, and she wasn't afraid of working out with the black belts in class. Her ukemi seemed solid and she took falls and rolls with confidence.

One class, Sensei showed a technique that I'd never done before. It was Hiji Dori, where Uke grabbed their partner's right elbow with their right hand, then moved behind them to grab the left elbow with their left hand. Then Nage scooted backwards, in toward Uke, and pivoted their front foot, then threaded their head through their arms so that Uke's arms were now in front of them. If this sounds complex, it was. Imagine me trying this with a few weeks of practice under my stiff white belt. Whew.

I grabbed Linda-san's right elbow and went around behind her to grab her left elbow. She did the technique and we started again.

The third time, I grabbed her elbow and she pivoted. But as her face turned toward me, she whispered, "If you don't stop pinching me, what goes around comes around."

I didn't have much experience, but I could feel the energy behind her words. It wasn't a suggestion for a beginner to learn how to grab properly. It was a whispered threat that retaliation was coming, and she meant business.

My hands dropped from her elbows to my sides.

"Oh, I'm so sorry!" I whispered back. We don't talk on the mat; that's part of our dojo's etiquette. Practice is for practicing techniques, not talking about them, and certainly not "teaching" and giving pointers to the other student – that is Sensei's job.

But I whispered one more thing. "I didn't know I was hurting you. I'm so sorry."

At that moment, Sensei called "Yame," which means "end." It's the signal for students to stop the technique they're working on, bow to their partner, say Arigatou Gozaimasu, and kneel in seiza at the edge of mat, ready to watch the next technique. This entire transition takes about seven seconds once you know what's expected.

The rest of the night, Linda-san worked with other people. I admit I wasn't sad about that.

I drove home thinking about what happened. I felt so bad, so guilty. I didn't mean to cause Linda-san pain. I had no idea how my grab was hurting her. It certainly was not my intent. But it had, and I needed to learn to do better.

In the next class, I was ready to try the Hiji Dori technique again. I'd been mentally reviewing how I'd grabbed and could feel that maybe I'd used too much thumb pressure and that was causing the pinching.

Instead, Sensei focused the class on Katate Dori techniques – grabbing the Nage's hand with the opposite hand. So, Nage would offer their right hand, and Uke would grab with their left.

We started with Katate Dori Shiho Nage, a technique we'd done several times over the past few months. Nage steps off the line but keeps their grabbed hand in place, as if a metal pole is holding it to the ground. At the same time, their free hand captures Uke's hand, so Nage's arms cross in an X in front of them.

Then, Nage enters the space as they bring Uke's hand to their head and pivot underneath it. This bends Uke's arm at the elbow and allows their hand and forearm to come to the side of their own head. Nage brings Uke's hand toward the side of their head and follows through with a throw like a sword cut.

I worked with John-san for the first technique and was getting the general hang of it.

"Yame," said Sensei.

Linda-san and I bowed toward each other. We begain by saying "Onegaishimasu."

Being my Sempai, Linda-san offered her right hand. I grabbed it with my left. She cut through the space, pivoted and brought her hand to her head, bringing my elbow up and my arm to my head. She kept the grip as she was supposed to do, following the arc of a sword cut as she finished the technique.

All felt good to me. We finished her next three techniques, and then it was my turn. For four techniques, I did my best to do the technique.

On the next round, Linda-san did her first technique. As she brought my hand to her head, just before the throw, she whispered.

"God, you're so short," she said. "It's such a pain to work with you."

In the years that would follow, I'd hear variations of comments on how short I was from many people, but it was said kindly and we'd share the joke together. Linda-san didn't say it as a joke or in a friendly, kidding way. Her comment had teeth, veiled repercussions that I'd pay for her discomfort caused by my height.

I took the ukemi – a side fall – and then stood up. I grabbed her outreached arm again, and I said nothing.

I knew right then that I might have some control over inadvertently pinching my partner in the Hiji Dori technique from the class before. But I had zero control of how tall I was.

From then on, I did my best to work willingly with Linda-san when we were partners. I used the opportunity to explore each technique. Feel the movement. Improve my ukemi. Improve my technique. Finish our round of techniques and move on to my next partner for the class.

But I decided right then to not let her comments derail me or to take them personally. I just kept training and being respectful.

**Your Turn**: You may want to take a bit of time to answer the following questions. They may help you capture and explore your own thoughts as they relate to the concepts from this chapter of the journey.

Is there a person in your life who reacted with anger or frustration when you least expected it? Has there been a situation that took you completely by surprise? What happened?

Is there a situation where you're faced with making the decision to continue something you enjoy doing, in spite of another person's actions? Which path will you choose – continue or stop?

Can you explore what happened and see if this situation is more about the other person than you? This doesn't mean not taking responsibility for your part in the interaction. But if something is said or done completely out of the blue, consider why.

Can you shift the perspective and see that perhaps what looks like animosity or mean-spirited comments or actions may be coming from a place of vulnerability or pain? Does that help you deal with the situation in a different way?

# 己達せんと欲して
# 人を達せしむ

*(Onore tassen to hosshite*
*hito o tasseshimu.)*

If you wish to succeed,
first help others to do the
same.

# 09 Becoming Part of Something Bigger Than Yourself

We moved the dojo to the YMCA and started practice there on Friday nights and Saturday mornings.

Before every class, we carried the Zebra grappling mats from the little closet that was about 30 feet down the indoor running track and tucked into the corner. With each mat weighing about 60 lbs., we all developed our own signature way of carrying them. The goal was to balance the mat on one side of your body with one hand underneath the midpart of the mat and the other hand overhead. It really wasn't too hard once you got the hang of it.

After class, we'd pick up the mats from the wood floor of our dojo room and carry them back to the closet. This took a bit more finesse than simply pulling the mats off the stack in the closet. The technique I used to pick up a mat was to tip the mat onto its front corner, then slide my hand half way underneath and pick it up so it rested on that same shoulder.

The higher the stack of mats grew in the closet, the more hip power we needed to hoist the mats onto the pile. For me, it was like stacking hay bales.

An added bonus to moving the mats in and out of the closet every class was the sense of timing it developed. Dodging the runners and walkers on the track became a dance, and moving the mats became an exercise in motion, timing, and blending.

With our practice now settling into a new routine, I started noticing something. We didn't have a big dojo – maybe 10 people if everyone was on the mat. But that's the thing. Even with only 10 people, there came to be a small core of students who showed up. Les-san, John-san, Cory-san, Keith-san, Bob-san, and I were usually there. Linda-san was getting sporadic, as were Russ-san and Dave-san.

The thing I realized was that Sensei was there every class. Every single class. I felt that the least I could do was to be there every single class as well. While I wasn't used as his Uke to demonstrate a technique very often, I was there to practice with the other students.

I also realized that we students needed each other to practice with. Aikido needs a training partner. Yes, you can practice the elements of movements by yourself (as I practiced Tai no Henko in the kitchen while waiting for the pasta water to boil) but to practice the blending, timing, entering, and spatial awareness of Aikido, we needed partners.

While I may have been a beginner, I was at least a partner to practice with. I realized that showing up to class was for our individual benefit to learn Aikido, but I began to see how showing up benefited everyone in the class.

**Your Turn**: You may want to take a bit of time to answer the following questions. They may help you capture and explore your own thoughts as they relate to the concepts from this chapter of the journey.

What is an activity in your life that needs a partner?

What's an area where your presence (not necessarily your talent or ability) aids the efforts of the group?

Is there an activity you do that needs the interaction of others to be helpful? Some ideas could be a book group, a writing group, pickup basketball, touch football? How do you feel when others don't show up?

# 塵も積もれば
# 山となる

*(Chiri mo tsumoreba yama to naru.)*

Even dust amassed will grow into a mountain.

# 10 Consistency

As winter turned into spring, practice continued at the YMCA. Like the tick of a metronome, practice developed a rhythm.

We arrived at the Y. We put on our keiko gi in the locker rooms. We climbed two flights of stairs past the front reception area. We moved the mats in. We bowed in to class. We practiced. We bowed out of class. We moved the mats out. We changed out of our gis in the locker rooms. We met outside the dojo to be sure everyone was healthy and safe. We said goodnight.

We arrived at the next practice and repeated the steps again.

This consistency punctuated my life and added form and shape to my weeks and months. Aikido wasn't something I fit in if I didn't have anything else going on. Instead, I fit the rest of my life around my practice. After all, we only practiced twice a week. If I missed those, I knew my learning wouldn't progress, and I needed all the practice I could get to continue to have tiny improvements.

I'm not sure why, but soon after I began to practice, I started a tracking log. It was just a sheet of paper with dates of practices for the month.

I also started a journal of what I learned in every class.

When I got home after each class, I wrote down the techniques we'd practiced and any tips or light-bulb moments I had. There were lots after most classes. Then, I added another tic mark to my practice log. Nothing excited me more than seeing the numbers add up. Pretty soon, I had 15 classes. Then 25.

Then 50! I'd attended 50 Aikido classes! Looking at my tic marks gave me a thrill, and seeing the numbers grow excited me more than I can really explain.

I realized that each class might not have a breakthrough or a significant increase in ability or understanding. But without each class, this deeper understanding didn't even have a chance of happening.

I knew that each class would be what it needed to be – whether that was confusion or clarity. Both got me farther along the journey. And in the end, the goal wasn't about improvement. It was about consistency.

I realized I had developed a Practice with a capital "P."

The Practice of Aikido shaped my life and gave me stepping stones through the days and weeks and years. And it gave me the grounding points to anchor me through the big challenges that lay ahead.

**Your Turn**: You may want to take a bit of time to answer the following questions. They may help you capture and explore your own thoughts as they relate to the concepts from this chapter of the journey.

What's something you'd like to develop a Practice around? It can be starting your day with a 10-minute walk around the block or drinking 60 oz. of water each day. Your Practice doesn't need to take a long time or be a huge effort. In fact, it's better if it's quick, short, and doable. No matter what happens in your day, this Practice is a grounding point.

Is there an activity you used to do that you want to explore again and develop a Practice around it?

Developing "streaks" of doing something daily triggers dopamine in our brain and rewards us for our action. Can you develop a simple tracker that shows your consistency with your Practice?

# 人生山あり谷あり

*(Jinsei yama ari tani ari.)*

# Life has mountains and valleys.

# 11 What's Known Is No Longer

It was a soft spring day in early May. The winter's snow had finally gone, and the weather warming into summer left Sedalia looking like Ireland. The hills everywhere were bright green with lush grass. New leaves on the aspen and willows and scrub oak peeked out, giving them a faint green aura. In a few weeks, they'd be fully enrobed in shades of green.

I got home from work and changed into my riding clothes. With the snow and mud of winter gone, it was time for Eddie and me to enjoy more riding time. We didn't have an arena, so we practiced what I called "road dressage" on the shoulders of the dirt roads around the neighborhood.

Certain places were good for practicing leg yields and two tracking movements, with either Eddie's front legs or back legs moving off the straight line he was walking. Other places were perfect for practicing our transitions from walk or trot to canter. A few places were wide and open to play with serpentines and circles, keeping the curves round and symmetrical. And mostly, our rides were simply joy at spending time together, in nature, walking past the scrub oak groves and shaded by pines, smelling the air of each season and watching the colors change to meet them.

Our riding times followed a similar pattern. When I'd round the corner of the back garage and slip through the gate leading down the short dirt lane to the barn, Eddie would see me and lift his head. Eyes bright. Ears up. I'd been spotted. Then he'd whinny. A big, loud, exuberant whinny, greeting me with "Hello, friend!"

Then he'd trot up to meet me and I gave him a hug. My face buried in the curve of his strong, brown neck, I took in the smell of

Eddie. The smell of Equus, of connection, of presence. It was the best smell in the world and I never got tired of it.

He dipped his nose into the black halter that brought out the handsomeness of his mahogany brown coat and black forelock, mane, and tail. We walked side by side to the gate, I let us through, and closed it behind us. Serena the donkey was always sad we were leaving her behind, and let out a soft bray.

I'd have his saddle, pad, and bridle waiting on the front deck, and I clipped his halter to a tie rope I'd fastened around one of the sturdy pine trees that ringed the front driveway. We didn't need a fancy barn or tie rack. Our outdoor tack room was just fine.

That's how our rides usually started.

But on this warm late afternoon, I rounded the corner of the garage. Eddie was standing out in front of the barn. He raised his head and pricked up his ears when he saw me. Eddie whinnied, but it was a very different whinny. It wasn't the greeting for a friend. It sounded more like a cry for help. He didn't come to meet me.

"What's up, buddy?" I called to him as I walked down the lane. Something was wrong, but he looked just fine. I didn't see any wounds, he wasn't holding up a leg. Serena was fine, poking her head out from the big run-in shed they shared.

And then I got closer. Looking down at his left front hoof, I could see why he'd called for help. Where strong hoof wall had been, now there was none. The entire outside half of his hoof was gone, exposing the soft, bloody flesh underneath. His forelegs were splattered with dried blood. The wound wasn't fresh, but as traumatic as it was, the active bleeding had slowed.

"Oh, Eddie," I said softly.

I put my hand on his neck and he curled his head toward me. I swear I heard him say, "I'm glad you're here. I need your help."

I knelt down to get a closer look to see the extent of the injury and to see if he had other cuts from whatever had happened.

There were none. Just the missing hoof wall on his left front.

I gave him a hug. "I'll be right back, Eddie. Don't worry."

I ran up to the house and called Dr. Streeter. Our vet was one of the best, and kindest, I'd ever known. His wife Kathi was his vet tech, and I loved them both for their expertise and their compassion.

Kathi answered the mobile number and I described what had happened. They were finishing up a call not too far away and would be to my house in about 30 minutes.

I went back down to the barn and hooked up the hose. Initial common practice with horse wounds is to flush with cold water, lots of water. It helps remove any dirt, the cold water helps the swelling, and it helps the injury to stop bleeding.

I knew Eddie didn't need to be haltered and I didn't need to hold or tie him. He stood as I started the water streaming down his hoof, lifting it off the ground a few inches, then putting it down as he adjusted to the initial shock of the water. But he didn't move from the place he was standing. I couldn't imagine the pain. It'd be like me ripping off every toenail on my left foot. But I'd be lucky. My toenails didn't bear the weight of my body.

When Dr. Streeter and Kathi arrived, they walked down to the barn carrying supplies in a stainless steel bucket.

"So what kind of mischief did you get into, Eddie?" Dr. Streeter asked in his quiet voice, then reached out his hand and Eddie touched it with his nose. His hand moved gently up to caress Eddie's face, and then slid down his neck where it stayed as he took the initial look.

The bleeding was mostly stopped and the hosing had made clear where the hoof wall had been ripped off like a piece of cardboard. Hoof material is about ½ inch thick, and it's as hard as linoleum. The amount of force it took to do this was inconceivable.

Kathi put the halter on Eddie because cleaning the wound would be excruciating. They knew he was a great patient, but putting his halter on might give him a sense of security and also keep everyone safe.

Dr. Streeter palpated each leg to be sure there were no broken bones or internal injuries. He asked Eddie to walk a couple feet to see if he was sound. He took a step, limping from the pain, but was willing to walk with encouragement. That was a good sign.

"Eddie is one stoic horse," said Dr. Streeter. "Most horses with this level of injury wouldn't be able to walk at all, or they'd be three-legged lame. He's a tough guy. And he's a good guy."

Dr. Streeter gave Eddie a shot of pain reliever and a sedative. He snipped away the ragged edges of hoof wall and then cleaned the wound and set his hoof gently down on a rubber mat to keep it clean and off the ground.

"You ready to learn hoof wrapping 101?" asked Dr. Streeter as he gave me a slight smile. "You're gonna be a pro soon, because Eddie will need to have his foot bandaged until the hoof grows in – and that'll take about a year."

In a few minutes, Eddie's hoof was completely encased, starting with a thick, sterile no-stick pad over the wound held in place with red roll gauze wrapped in figure eights around the entire hoof. Next, vet-wrap circled up and down from the fetlock and around the hoof.

Finally, a thick base of two layers of duct tape was applied to the bottom of the hoof to protect the wrapping from shredding when he walked.

Eddie breathed a big exhale. It must have felt so much better to not have that raw flesh exposed to the air. With a tetanus booster and a shot of antibiotics, Eddie was good to go.

I walked up the lane with Dr. Streeter and Kathi, and got final instructions and a bunch of gauze and pads and wraps to get me started. After they cleaned up and put the supplies into their truck – a vet clinic on wheels – they both gave me a hug.

"You'll do great, and we all know Eddie's an amazing patient."

I nodded, "He sure is."

Eddie was an amazing patient as we started the long road to recovery. In a few months as the hoof started growing back and filling in the void, I was able to start putting on a hoof boot instead of the full bandage wrap. This also meant Eddie was able to go out to the back pasture and graze with Serena, which made him very happy.

In a year, his hoof fully grew back. From the outside, you couldn't tell which hoof had been injured. It was strong, smooth. But on the bottom of the hoof, there was always a gap that couldn't grow in.

Eddie was sound in the pasture, able to walk, trot, and canter without being lame. One day, it was time to see if we could ride again. We saddled up and headed out the driveway at a slow walk. Eddie's head started bobbing a bit in time with his injured hoof. He was lame.

Dr. Streeter said to try again a few times. Just saddle up and go for a short, gentle walk. See if his hoof is able to adjust to the added pressure of riding.

We tried a few more times, and every time, Eddie was lame.

The last time, I pulled off his saddle and groomed him. And then I put my arms around his strong, brown neck and cried.

"All right, my friend," I whispered. "You're retired. And I'll take care of you for the rest of your days."

**Your Turn**: You may want to take a bit of time to answer the following questions. They may help you capture and explore your own thoughts as they relate to the concepts from this chapter of the journey.

Have you experienced a sudden trauma, to someone you love or yourself, that changed the future? What was it?

If you're in the middle of dealing with the event, what can you do to stay present and do what needs to be done while remaining optimistic?

Do you need help to get through the trauma? Who can help you?

# 情けに刃向かう
# 刃なし

*(Nasake ni hamukau
yaiba nashi.)*

# No sword can oppose
# kindness.

# 12 Allowing in Truth

The cool of the vinyl grappling mat pressed on my right cheek. My left arm was pointing up to the ceiling, pinned tight to Les-san's chest as he did the final pin of a Sankyo Ura technique.

Pinned to the mat, there was nowhere I could go. I couldn't bend my arm. I couldn't even move my hand. I certainly couldn't stand up.

The weeks of Aikido Practice had turned into months and the months into nearly two years. The rhythm of Aikido was the rhythm of my life.

As I lay there, in those few seconds of soothing coolness, a knowing seeped into every part of me.

Here was Les-san, pinning me to the mat. There was John-san working with Linda-san. There was Keith-san pinning Dave-san, and Russ-san, Bob-san and Cory-san working in a group of three. And there was Sensei, teaching and guiding us as we practiced.

There was strong martial spirit. There was a committed attack from Uke. There was the intention from Nage to do the technique correctly. There was focus and intensity.

But nowhere was there anger.

Nowhere was there frustration or harsh words. Class was consistent, respectful, and most of all, safe. The focus, the mood, the energy didn't change depending on Sensei's mood or what kind of a day he was having.

Nowhere was there a quickness to anger, but often there was a quickness to laughter, or at least a smile, from almost everyone in class.

In those few seconds, I realized that my life outside the dojo was completely different.

My experience at home was anticipation and dread. I waited for the flip of the light switch from happy to rage. I lived daily with the feeling of walking on eggshells, not knowing when the mood would change, doing all I could to prevent it. And still, all my attempts at being kind and helpful and understanding… and then very, very quiet… did nothing to stop the rage from returning.

I never knew what each day would bring, or "which" John would walk in the door after work. Would it be the happy and often funny John? Or the John who was mad, ready to throw things, scream at me, call me vile names, and say that it was my fault: if I didn't provoke him, he wouldn't get so angry?

I never knew what would happen next, and I couldn't predict. All I did know was that I was living in a continual state of dread and instability. To make sense of the ever-shifting environment, I'd begun to rationalize that every marriage must have these very dark and scary times. We all got married "for good or for bad," right? This must be the bad stuff, and since it must happen to everyone, no one talked about it.

But somehow in those few seconds of pause, pinned completely to the mat, a tiny piece of the veil that had covered so many days lifted. The tiniest corner pulled up and light poured in.

"These men…," I heard a small voice begin to say. "I bet these men don't treat their wives the way I'm treated. I bet these men, all strong and powerful, don't scream at their wives and call them names. I bet they don't break things, or threaten, or belittle the people they say they love."

The small, but strong, voice of my wise soul continued. "I bet these men don't do the things I live in fear of and the daily instability that comes from not knowing what the day will bring."

And maybe, just maybe, I could choose to live a life that doesn't have these things in it any more. A life of peace, calm, consistency. Maybe I don't know if I can change things, but I do know that the life I'm living is killing me. My soul dies a bit more every day.

This unspoken dialogue was more a sense, a knowing, than actual words. As Les-san released the pin, the voice stopped.

I stood up. I moved in to strike Shomen Uchi to his head, and the next technique started.

Class finished, just like every class before it. We bowed out, thanked our partners, changed out of our gis, and drove home.

But the person I was when I bowed into class was not the same person who bowed out.

**Your Turn**: You may want to take a bit of time to answer the following questions. They may help you capture and explore your own thoughts as they relate to the concepts from this chapter of the journey.

Is there a piece of your life, large or small, that you know is not what you want?

Is there a situation or a person whose presence brings you down, threatens you, overwhelms you, or frightens you?

Can you use the mirror of your Practice to shine into you the truth of your life? With this light of clarity, what no longer serves you?

What are some areas in your life you would like to change? Maybe not right away, or maybe not with huge changes right now, but areas where you can take a step toward changing, improving, or letting go?

Is there something that is calling to you or that you'd like to move toward?

# 先のことは
# 分からない

*(Saki no koto wa
wakaranai.)*

# What lies ahead is
# unknown.

# 13 Courage

The next year of Practice went by, as I checked off class after class in my tracking sheet. The movements and techniques were slowly becoming part of me and my muscle memory. No longer completely foreign, the techniques started deepening and becoming my own. Oh, I had miles to go on this life journey, but the basics were settling in to my body and mind.

Along the way, I'd been promoted through the white belt ranks from 6th kyu (Rokkyu) to 5th kyu (Gokyu) to 4th kyu (Yonkyu). Then one day, I was promoted to Sankyu rank, the first of three brown belt ranks.

That class started like every other class. Sensei bowed us in, we did warmups, then started practicing. Within a few techniques, however, I realized we were being asked to do the techniques for my next rank test.

I was being tested.

After the next technique, Sensei asked John-san to be my partner. We practiced a few more of my techniques. Sensei told us to keep practicing and not change partners.

I had a feeling that John-san was being tested, too. His next level would be Shodan – first degree black belt.

"John-san, let's see six techniques from Shomen Uchi," Sensei instructed. I attacked John-san with a strong overhead strike.

"Good. Now, Kara-san, you do four."

This continued for several different attacks, with John-san doing techniques first and then me.

"Hai. Yame," called Sensei.

All of us students kneeled in seiza at the edge of the mat, waiting for the next technique.

"We're going to end class with some Randori," he said. "Ukes for John-san will be Les-san, Cory-san, and Kara-san."

John-san moved to the right edge of the mat and we lined up opposite him.

"Start when you're ready, John-san."

"Hajime!" John-san called out as he bowed to us and quickly stood up. We ran in to attack. He moved in and responded to each attack, throwing us different directions, slipping through an opening, using the space, staying aware of his attackers' location, not getting trapped.

"Hai! Yame!" Sensei called again. "Thank your partners, then final line."

John-san returned to the edge of the mat and we Ukes returned to the other. We bowed, then we lined up in rank order to end the class.

The four of us who had just finished Randori were breathing hard.

"John-san, please come up," Sensei motioned to the space next to him in front of the Shomen.

He reached behind the Shomen and pulled out a new black belt. I could see it was monogrammed.

He laid it in front of him on the mat. "John-san, you've been training hard and consistently. Your Aikido is developing really well. And you're a great Sempai in our dojo."

He picked up the new belt and held it out to John-san with both hands. "You are now promoted to the rank of Shodan. Omedetou gozaimasu, John-san." John-san turned and bowed to us. I clapped hard with the rest of the students. I was so proud of John-san! He'd helped me so much with my Practice, including meeting at the park for lots of weapons practices.

Sensei reached behind the Shomen and pulled out a new brown belt.

"Kara-san," he said. "Please come up."

I knee-walked up to the Shomen and sat in seiza facing Sensei.

He placed the brown belt in front of him. Monogrammed in black were the kanji for Kiryu Aikido and my name in katakana. Ka Ra.

"You have come so far since you started training, Kara-san," he said.

"Your consistency and dedication are inspiring to everyone in the dojo, and your techniques are getting strong."

He held up the belt with both hands, bowing as he handed it to me. "You are now promoted to the rank of Sankyu. Omedetou gozaimasu. Congratulations, Kara-san."

I bowed deeply and received the belt with both hands. "Doumo arigatou gozaimasu, Sensei."

I turned and bowed to the students and thanked them as well.

I was in shock. While I thought that someday I might be promoted if I kept practicing and improving, I certainly did not expect this. And especially not tonight.

I was humbled and grateful for all the help I'd been given by Sensei and my Sempai.

Classes continued. More focus, more consistency. Practice after practice, week after week.

Several months later, Sensei shared that we would be testing with Tanshinjuku and several other dojos in the fall. As had been the case with my prior promotions, we normally did internal testing at Kiryu. Now, however, we were going to be testing with Izawa Sensei. We'd also now receive our ranks through Aikikai, the International Aikido Federation in Japan.

After class, Sensei shared that he was recommending me to test for Nikyu – the second degree of our brown belt ranks.

I bowed and said, "Hai, Sensei." I'd been training hard, and I would do everything I could to be ready.

<hr />

The morning of my Nikyu test in September 2008, the sun came up like it always did. But the day was vastly different, and not only because I had a large milestone test ahead of me.

The night before, John had gone off the deep end with anger. The discussion had started calmly about the upcoming hunting season.

I'd always gone with him. During the day when he was out hunting, I'd stay at camp and read, write, do yoga, go for walks. It was quiet time and I enjoyed it.

Earlier that summer, I'd taken several days of vacation to attend a weeklong horse training seminar with Mark Rashid. When John asked about hunting this year, I said sure I'd like to go. Then I added casually that I just needed to see how much vacation I had. With the clinic, I wasn't sure if I had enough to be gone the full week. I figured at least I could go for part of hunting camp, and we could drive two cars if I needed to come back earlier.

For some reason that's likely deeper than I knew, John blew up. My matter-of-fact statement met rage.

He screamed at me. He said I'd promised and now I was breaking that promise. I tried to calm him down. I tried to explain that I didn't say no. I just had to find out how much vacation I had.

Like so many other times, nothing I said would change anything. And anything I said was twisted and shouted over and served as fuel for more anger. I tried to say I wanted to go. That we could take two cars. That I would be there for at least part of the trip. But those words hung in the air like icicles on the eaves, then fell to the ground and shattered.

He slept in the guest room that night. Even with all the anger and horrendous outbursts over the years, it was the first time this had ever happened in 22 years of marriage.

I slept fitfully. Swirling and mist and a shrouded path dominated my dreams. When I awoke in the morning, I hoped that the pain, deep misunderstanding, and hard words of the night before had been the real dream.

I looked over to John's side of the bed. He wasn't there. I knew then the nightmare had been real.

I got up and made coffee. Sitting at the kitchen table, I thought about the night before and the awfulness of it. The divide between us, John's inability to hear that I would make it to camp somehow, the pain I was causing even though that was the furthest thing from my intent, the pain he was exhibiting.

I hoped the night apart had healed the bad feelings. Maybe we could just start over with a rational conversation about logistics.

Then I thought about the day ahead. The testing started at 9:00. I had a choice.

I could go. Or I could decide not to go – tell Sensei something big had happened.

John wandered into the kitchen. I said good morning. Silence.

I started to reassure him I wanted to go to hunting camp and we'd make it work. He was having none of it. The conversation escalated

again into anger and rage, cutting me off, not letting me explain, shouting over me.

Looking back, now I can understand the fear and the pain he was feeling. I always went with him. Always. The possibility of me not going was deeper than missing a hunting trip. It must have felt like the unraveling was moving more quickly as the wedge of pain and fear between us grew and grew.

He knew things were changing. And his only way to cope, to stop the pulling of the thread, was to explode.

I got another cup of coffee and sat down. He went outside to get the newspaper.

Would missing my test save my marriage? Would going to my test end my marriage? I considered each option, each outcome. The answer was the same. My choice had nothing to do with the future of my marriage.

I'd spent 22 years acquiescing, letting his decisions overshadow mine, saying no to my dreams because he didn't approve, allowing my soul to shrivel and die in the life of fear and chaotic inconsistency that was my existence. Too weak to stand up for myself, too scared to say anything. I'd lost my voice and my way and my light. It wasn't all John's fault. He coped with rage. I coped with quiet.

Now what? Which path would I choose?

John came in and sat down at the kitchen table, opening the newspaper.

I started making breakfast. "Would you like some eggs? I'm happy to make you some."

I just wanted things to be better.

That question just brought more anger. "No, I don't want breakfast!" his voice boomed.

"If you'd just do what you'd promised, what we agreed to, I wouldn't have to get so mad all the time!"

I made myself breakfast and John went into the living room.

I could hear the snapping of the newspaper as he flipped to a new page.

I cleaned up the kitchen and packed my gi bag. I walked into the living room and took a breath.

"I'll be back after the tests," I said. "And I heard that people might go to lunch afterwards; I'll let you know where if you want to come."

Silence.

As I drove to the dojo, I didn't know what I'd find when I got back. I didn't know if I'd have a marriage when I got back. I didn't know if John would still be in the house. I didn't know if he'd pack up his things and leave. I didn't know if he'd throw my things out on the front porch. I didn't know if he'd destroy things I cherished, like Grandma's piano or the animals I loved.

Or if we'd finally be able to have a conversation that could build a path to a better future and the life I'd always wanted with John: peaceful, supportive, happy. A conversation that didn't end with the phrase he pulled out of the verbal holster so often I'd lost track: "I'm not changing. If you don't like it, let's just get divorced."

All I did know was that I'd reached a line in the sand. I could not go back to what I had, and I'd gained enough strength in my Practice the past two years for me to, finally, stand firm for something that I wanted more than anything. My mental health.

For the rest of the drive, I visualized my test. Moving confidently from technique to technique. Filling each moment with martial spirit and focus. Flowing through the test with ease.

Arriving at the dojo, I changed into my gi. My friend Katie from California was there to watch my test. I was so touched and honored that she'd made the effort to be there.

The dojo was filling up with students and Senseis, family and friends. We'd be seeing many tests today.

After warmups, we all lined up in seiza at the back of the mat. The Senseis from each dojo lined up in seiza facing the shomen.

"Rei." We all bowed to the Shomen.

"Onegaishimasu." We students bowed to the Senseis.

The tests began. We started with the young children at lower ranks from another dojo. Then the lower-level adult students tested, starting with Gokkyu and moving into higher ranks as the tests went on.

Finally, it was my turn. "Kara-san and Uke, testing for Nikyu," called out Sensei. Keith-san was my Uke. We stood up, walked to the opposite ends of the mat, bowed to each other, walked to the center of mat, and kneeled in seiza facing the portrait of our founder O-Sensei and the Shomen.

"Shomen ni rei," I said in my strongest, most martial voice. This meant "bow to the front of the dojo." We bowed to O-Sensei.

"Sensei ni rei." This meant "bow to the Sensei." We bowed in turn to Izawa Sensei, Blevins Sensei, and Albright Sensei.

"Ota gai ni rei." This meant "bow to each other." Keith-san and I turned and bowed to each other.

I don't remember much about the techniques during my test.

What I do remember is the endless gratitude I felt to be there. Present in this moment. Savoring the opportunity to do something that brought me joy. Sharing time with people who shared the path. Grateful for my health and my life and the journey that had brought me to Here and wherever it would lead me to next.

I knew this moment was all I had. It's all any of us had. The past was done. The future was out of our control. This moment was all that mattered.

**Your Turn**: You may want to take a bit of time to answer the following questions. They may help you capture and explore your own thoughts as they relate to the concepts from this chapter of the journey.

Courage takes all shapes and forms. It deals with facing What Is rather than hiding, fighting, resisting the present moment, or worrying about What If.

Do you have a place in your life that's taking courage to face? Are you facing a reality that may be different from the one you'd always assumed would be your future?

Are you coming to a crossroads with a situation or a person? Did you see it coming?

When you envision the future, what's the outcome you'd like to have? How can you prepare?

# 継続は力なり

*(Keizoku wa chikara nari.)*

Continuance is power.
Continuing becomes
strength.

# 14 Strength

After the tests were over, we all went out to lunch to celebrate as a community. While I was happy about my test and passing it, and grateful for the time with teachers and fellow students, I was distracted. I didn't know what would be waiting for me when I got home.

When I arrived, John was in the garage changing the oil in the truck. I tried to talk... talk one more time about my desire to have a better future. Doing better together. The night before could be a turning point. We could start a new path.

I opened the door again to counseling. I had asked many times before, several times a year. He had always said no. No way.

This time, he agreed. I was so surprised, and so glad. I wanted nothing more than to be happy, together. To live our lives supporting each other's dreams and sharing our lives with love, laughter, joy.

A few days later, he said no. No way. Counseling was for the weak. Strong people figured things out themselves, he said.

I think the "no" meant facing change that would need to run deep, to the core. I flashed back to that summer a few years before, sitting with John on the back porch. I had a yellow note pad on my lap. I'd asked gently to have a conversation about what each of us needed and explore together how we could do that. It seemed simple – the notion of asking your partner for what you need and your partner lovingly, willingly trying to give you that. And vice versa.

This wasn't to be a conversation of demands, blame, judgment. I envisioned two people who loved each other coming together to support the other in kindness, respect, and with a willing heart.

I went first. This was so hard for me, to ask for what I needed. But I took a deep breath and started.

"I'd like to ask to not be called names," I said quietly. "It really hurts me when you call me names during an argument. I'd like to have discussions and conversations about whatever's bothering us, and then work together and come up with solutions that work for both of us."

It seemed quite simple to me, and a very reasonable request between a husband and wife. I paused, expecting John to share his request of what he'd like from me.

"I can't do that," he said. "I can't promise not to call you names."

I put the pen down on the yellow pad and looked out to the horizon, past the ring of pine trees circling the back yard and far out to the ridge of hills leading up the canyon to Pike National Forest.

I didn't know what to say. There was nothing to say.

I let the reality sink in.

My most basic request – to not be called names – couldn't be met. My desire to have a relationship of mutual respect and care for the other person's needs couldn't be a reality.

I'd seen the writing on the wall many times over the years, but still I'd chosen to stay, to hope, to work on having a marriage of friendship and support, doing all I could to change things.

But with John's final, solid syllable of "no" to getting help so we could be better together, I knew the door to hope had slammed shut.

I knew finally in my heart there was no way to fix this, not on my own. I also sadly knew that sharing this decision as an ultimatum – either we get counseling or I need to leave – was pointless. It would only create rage and I wanted John to choose working together because he wanted a better life together. Not to be forced into change because he was backed into a corner.

I also knew how volatile he was. I'd seen so many times over the years the light switch flip from calm to absolute rage in seconds. I knew that to protect me and my horses and my dog, I had to leave in the cover of daylight. There would sadly be no conversation about me leaving, no sharing that one person couldn't fix us, no acknowledging that he wasn't happy and I couldn't make him so. No kind wish that maybe he'd have a chance to find happiness without me.

A few days later, I walked up the dirt road to Mary's house. She was going to be out of town for a few days and asked if I could feed her horses and dogs while she gone. I stopped in to get the details.

I knocked on the front door and the low woofs of three Basset Hounds greeted me. Mary opened the door and three bundles of loose skin, flopping ears, and happy faces bounded past me to the front yard.

We walked to the shed as her horses pricked up their ears at the visitors arriving. "Mary, can I talk to you about something?" I asked.

I knew she'd say yes. We shared a lot over the years – challenges, dreams, pain, joy – during our rides together or sitting at the kitchen table in their tidy house filled with animals and kindness.

With her former work in halfway houses and shelters, Mary knew how to listen and how to hear the feelings between the words. I remember one time asking if marriage was supposed to be so hard and so painful, so inconsistent you didn't know which end was up. I was reeling from another outburst that had come out of nowhere. Given the example I'd grown up with and parents who were truly best friends, I couldn't wrangle sense out of what I was experiencing in my marriage.

Some days, it was beautiful. Supportive, loving, calm, fun, and I couldn't imagine being happier. Other days, it was dark, scary; the world shifting and turning and swirling and all sense of balance was gone. I didn't know when the ground would fall from under my feet and when it would return, a solid place to stand once again… like nothing had happened. Maybe I'd been dreaming.

Did she experience this in her life? I asked for the truth. Maybe this pain and confusion was the "for bad" part of marriage we'd all signed up for. Maybe everyone had these tectonic shifts in their marriage but nobody talked about it. The thing was, even though I'd never seen this in my parent's marriage, I knew they weren't hiding it. I just knew it didn't happen with them. But the only way I could

rationalize my experiences as so off-kilter was to assume that darkness was part of marriage… and everybody knew that but me.

She'd said, no, this wasn't part of the contract, not part of the vows we took. If it was part of my life, I would know if and when it was time to change my part of the contract.

And when that day came, she would be there to help in whatever way I needed her. If I needed a safe place to go, her house and her pasture were open any time of day or night.

"Sure, what's up?" Mary asked. We stopped at the tie rack outside the pasture. Leaning one arm on the piece of telephone pole that had been cut down and repurposed into the solid place to tie her horses while she groomed them or saddled them up for a ride, Mary turned and waited.

I leaned both arms on the warm, rough wood and looked at her horses grazing quietly. I couldn't look at Mary. If I did, the words might not come out and the decision I'd made might not come to pass.

"I finally know I can't make our marriage better all by myself," I started. "I've tried, so many times, asking if we could do better, if we could work together to have a better marriage. I even went to counseling myself, and the counselor said to set boundaries of what was acceptable, but I'm too weak to enforce them and it's too scary to stand up to the anger."

I watched as Sadie the Basset Hound meandered through the tall autumn grass, snuffling her nose on the ground following the scent of some secret trail.

"I've made the decision that I need to leave John," I said. "I don't make him happy, and I'm dying inside more every day that I stay."

Mary came over and wrapped her arms around me. Now that the words were out, the tears started to fall.

"I'm starting to look for a place to rent that takes horses. There are a couple places on Craigslist that look like they could work, and I've made appointments to see them this week."

Over the next few weeks, I started looking at places to live. But none of them were right. Some were way beyond my budget, others didn't have a good place for Eddie and Serena. We didn't need fancy, but we needed safe and secure, a place to land for a while.

Then fate or serendipity or God intervened. Eva was a close friend of Mary's, and I'd met her several times. Eva had an energy and a spirit that buoyed people up, and if you didn't know she was an amputee, you'd never know by how active and self-sufficient she was. With several horses, dogs, and her gift shop to manage, she did it all while being there for her family and friends.

One warm afternoon, Mary and I stopped by Eva's to meet her big Percheron draft horse cross, Constantine. With Eddie being retired, Eva had wondered if I had an interest in buying him. I said I might.

As she let Constantine into the big pen, the three of us talked while we watched Constantine trot and canter around us. He certainly did have nice movement, and it seemed his athleticism might be a good fit for dressage training.

Conversation drifted to other things. Mary mentioned my situation and how I was leaving my marriage soon. Without missing a beat, Eva said, "You can live here."

I didn't know what to say. I knew Eva. The three of us had gone to horse events and tack sales and such over the years, but she and

Mary were the close friends. In the big scheme, Eva didn't really know me at all.

"I have a guest room, and you're welcome to it for as long as you need." She pointed to the stalls outside the big pen. "Eddie and Serena can share that space; it's big enough for two."

"Eva, really? You would do that?" I asked.

"Yes," she said. "Life can be a bitch; we all need to help each other out."

I agreed, the three of us hugged, and I started putting plans together to move myself and my horses in a couple weeks.

On a bright morning in late September, Mary, Eva, and Mary's sister Chris were waiting for the plan to unfold and to help me step into whatever lay ahead.

I went to work like any other day, but turned off the road and waited on a side street. After I saw John pass by on his way to work, I turned around and headed back home for the last time.

It only took us a couple hours to move the horses and the few things I was taking: clothes, my computer, my saddles, my Grandmother's piano. Moving the piano took the generosity and kindness of neighbors Vern and Larry.

I said goodbye to everything else, fully accepting that I would never see those things again. I was ok with that.

I left a note on the kitchen table. It was short. There was no point in sharing all the pain that had led up to this day.

"I don't make you happy. The horses and I are in a safe place. I'll contact you in a few days."

As I pulled the front door shut behind me, I also left with a soft heart and deep forgiveness. No anger. No blame. Just the light of truth lighting the way forward.

Whatever happened next, I had no control over it. Given John's rage, I fully expected the possibility of being stalked, killed, and that my horses would also be killed if he found them.

I also knew that no matter what happened, I was at peace. If I died trying to leave, it would still be worth trying to save my soul.

That afternoon, I sat in Eva's cozy, colorful house. As the sun got lower in the western sky, I packed up my gi bag and headed to Aikido.

I'd let my parents, Sensei, and Les-san know that I was leaving my marriage that day. I didn't give them details of where I'd be going, thinking it would be safer for everyone if they didn't know. I told my parents that I would call and let them know I was safe, and I told Sensei and Les-san that if I wasn't at class, something hadn't gone as planned.

As I put on my gi in the dressing room, my muscle memory tied the knot in the belt. My fingers found their way to tie the himo on my hakama. My brain was quiet yet not fully present after the events of the day. I walked up the stairs to the dojo and bowed inside the doorway.

Sensei and Les-san were there and asked, simply, "How are you?" I nodded ok, surprised at both the numbness and the tears that were threatening to spill out. I put down my gi bag and headed to the closet to help bring in the mats. The grey cool rectangles starting filling in the puzzle of the dojo floor.

Sensei bowed us in.

Rei. Onegaishimasu.

After warmups, he said tonight we'd be working on strikes.

"A committed attack is the most important part of Aikido. Without it, we can't practice," he shared.

Because the dojo was in a multi-purpose room, there were several free-standing punching bags around the edges of the mat.

"Kara-san," he said, pointing to one of the bags. "Practice your Yokomen strike."

I started striking the bag with the sideways angle of Yokomen and the triangle step that our footwork followed. Our aim in Yokomen is the temple of our attacker, someone the same height as we are.

My strikes were soft and tentative at first. I'd never used a punching bag.

"More intent, Kara-san," he said. "Committed attacks."

Tears stung as I struck harder, more on target. Following through with the correct angle.

We'd never used punching bags before, and we never did again. But that class, that night, Sensei knew what I needed. And he was right.

The weeks that followed were a blur. My normal had been upended. I took a different way to work. I left early and came home late to stay hidden. I didn't go see my parents, thinking it would be safer for them if I didn't.

The one thing that grounded me, gave me direction and a reason to keep going, was Aikido. I came to class. I put on my gi. I worked hard. I focused. And I made it to the next class, and the next and the next. Practice gave me a place to center, a place to simply breathe in, breathe out, move, and be.

**Your Turn**: You may want to take a bit of time to answer the following questions. They may help you capture and explore your own thoughts as they relate to the concepts from this chapter of the journey.

Is there an area in your life that's requiring you to dig deep and find your strength?

Is there a Practice that you can find grounding and centering in? What is that? How can you build it into your routine so you know it's always there for you?

Are there people or places that give you strength just by being in your life? Can you spend more time with them?

If you need to make a big change, who are people you can trust to help you through?

# 虎口を逃れて
# 竜穴に入る

*(Kokou o nogarete
ryuuketsu ni iru.)*

To escape a tiger's den
and enter the cave of the
dragon.

# 15 When it Rains...

I started to settle into my new life living in Eva's spare bedroom. Early each morning, I put on my headlamp and walked the gentle slope behind the house to feed the horses. Carrying Eddie's bucket of soaked food in one hand, I unlatched the gate and let myself in to the large pen.

After pouring Eddie's feed into the big rubber bucket, I went to the hay stack and loaded four flakes of hay into the cart to feed my horses and Eva's. One flake for Serena and Eddie to share, two for Constantine, one for the three miniature horses. Then I checked their water tanks to make sure the heaters were working and finished with scooping some of the manure into the large pen to be picked up later and put into the manure pile.

I let myself back in from the door off the kitchen, allowing the warmth and coziness of Eva's beautiful, art-filled house to embrace me, just like Eva did.

Eva was also an early riser and we had time for conversation and a warm cup – black tea with milk for Eva, coffee for me – before I left for work. Thanksgiving was just a few weeks away, and her gift shop was gearing up for the holiday shopping season. Months before, she'd ordered her inventory from the wholesale marts she attended and it was starting to arrive in big boxes of decorations, gifts, specialty food. Eva had an artist's eye for choosing the merchandise for her shop. Everything she chose was unique and appreciated by shoppers in her inviting store with its rustic lodge feel and the soul of nature, horses, and home.

Because I left for work early, often in the dark so there was less chance for John to see my truck pull out from the secluded space by the barn, I usually arrived at work before most of my coworkers.

That morning was no different, but I noticed the Human Resources manager talking to my manager Tom. That wasn't a normal thing.

There'd been whispers in the hall the past few weeks. The company had not won a huge contract it was betting on. Another large project was deeply in the red with cost and time overruns. In addition, the new president who'd stepped in after one of the founding members of the engineering firm retired as CEO was rumored to be considering layoffs to stop the financial bleeding.

But our team – web development and external communications – wasn't worried. We were tight, efficient, productive, and our work was often held up as a positive example in the company. For me, I was finally part of my dream team. We worked hard, we shared the same vision, we supported each other. Our work was engaging, fulfilling, and our team spirit infused us all with the confidence to stretch and grow and accomplish even more.

As more of my team started to arrive, there was a shift in the energy. The rumors were true. Today the company was laying off employees. How many remained to be seen.

Because I was one of the first ones in the office, I was one of the first called in to Tom's office. They started with how hard this was, how the company had been losing contracts, how the company needed to make the very hard and unfortunate decision to lay off valued staff so it could survive…. All the nonsense that they must say before they give you the paperwork to sign.

I heard the words. But they didn't really make sense. How could our team, our dream team, be broken apart?

I also was numb. Part of me couldn't believe that I'd just survived leaving my marriage – a scary, life-threatening situation – and now I was going to lose my job just a few weeks later. My brain flip-flopped from "how on earth can this be happening?" to "of course this is happening." And "what's next? Can things get any harder?"

I signed the papers and went to box up my cubicle. My direct manager Lee came over. He was nearly in tears. He had no input on who they let go. That morning when they told him, he fought to keep me and my other teammates. But to no avail. The faceless head count reduction in each team made sense on paper to HR and the accounting staff. And I was done.

Sitting in my truck with two boxes on the passenger seat, I felt nothing. I saw other coworkers start coming out of the building with their boxes. Our team had been decimated, and so had many others.

Later I heard that on the executive floor, when senior vice presidents and directors were called into the CEO's office to hear the same news, there was screaming. Profanity. Pounding of tables. "How could you?" these men yelled. "I've given my life to this company. I moved wherever you wanted me to, uprooted my family. Led any project you wanted me to take on and made it a success. And this? This is what I get?"

At the end of that day, hundreds of staff had been laid off. Every division, every business unit, every team had been affected.

I drove back to my new home at Eva's just a few hours after I'd left that morning. Large flakes of snow sprinkled from the gray sky. I pulled into the driveway and Eva was outside getting her mail.

She looked at me through the windshield, eyes wide and curious, mouthing the words, "what's up…?" She knew the news wasn't good that had brought me home on this cold November morning.

I hoisted a box from the passenger seat and met her in the warm house.

"I just got laid off," I said with an odd monotone to my voice. I still was numb. "They're doing massive layoffs today. I don't know how many of my friends will be gone, too."

"Oh, shit," she said, giving me a big hug. "I am so sorry. You did not need this, especially not right now."

I carried the other box into my bedroom while she made us tea. We sat on the couch and talked about what was ahead.

I'd get unemployment and I'd ramp up my freelance work again. That would tide me over until I found another job. In the meantime, I was looking forward to celebrating quiet holidays and getting over the shock.

I called my parents and shared the news with them. I'd come visit this weekend and couldn't wait to see them.

It was Friday – the best day to lay people off, according to studies by human resources organizations. On a Friday, there was less chance for employees to go off the deep end, to come into work the next day and do something catastrophic. On a Friday, the newly unemployed person could reach out to family and friends during the weekend ahead. Maybe go on a bender. Maybe celebrate. Maybe get really, really, really angry.

It was Friday. For me, Friday meant Practice at the dojo. A few hours later, I packed up my gi bag and headed to the YMCA.

I was more thankful than ever for my Practice… for the place to go where I could just be. Just breathe. Just move. Just Practice.

The next week, I asked Sensei if he would meet me for lunch. I had some questions about my training that I wanted his thoughts on.

We met at Three Margaritas. With plates of enchiladas steaming on the colorful table, I shared that I'd been thinking about being an Uchi Deshi (live-in student) somewhere and wanted his thoughts on whether this would be a good step for me.

I shared what I'd read: that an Uchi Deshi devotes him or herself fully to the position. Taking care of the needs of the Sensei and the dojo are the focus. Commitment to training – many hours a day – is expected.

He thought a moment before answering.

"You're right about the commitment and expectations," he said.

He'd been Uchi Deshi at dojos in Japan over the years. He spoke from experience.

He took a bite and paused. "It's a huge commitment," he said. "Being an Uchi Deshi means every moment of your day centers around the dojo."

Then he added, "And I think it would be a great experience for you. It's a huge challenge, but if you know what to expect and approach it the right way, the rewards are huge as well."

I took a few bites, letting what he said sink in.

"When I got laid off, I spent some time thinking about what was important to me and how I could use this as a door opening instead of a door closing. I've wanted to do this, and now I have the time."

"I think you'd really get a lot out of being Uchi Deshi," he said. "The time I spent as Uchi Deshi in Japan a few times was amazing. It can really change you as a person and deepen your training in a lot of ways."

"Ok," I said. "I definitely want to do this. Do you have any recommendations of which Senseis might be good for me to train with?"

"Yes, I have two," he answered immediately. "Pat Hendricks Sensei at Aikido of San Leandro in California or Stephanie Yap Sensei in Florida."

He added, "They're both very strong martial artists, good teachers, and have very high expectations. I respect them both and think they'd be a great fit."

I was so excited – and nervous. As we finished lunch, he said to look into the requirements for both dojos. He would write me a recommendation letter.

Hendricks Sensei's website had this description for those considering applying to be Uchi Deshi.

> *The dojo is the first priority. A person applying for uchi deshi status should understand that this commitment is not to be taken lightly. Although the rewards for one who totally immerses her/himself in Aikido training are great, the hardship of uchi deshi life can also be great. Everything is training. Living conditions are austere. The demands for the care and cleaning of the dojo and attention to the needs and wishes of the Sensei are unrelenting. Training is top priority in the life of an uchi deshi. This training is not only more demanding than that asked of the dojo members at large, but more frequent. For these reasons, one should consider very carefully before committing to a period of study as an uchi deshi.*

**Your Turn**: You may want to take a bit of time to answer the following questions. They may help you capture and explore your own thoughts as they relate to the concepts from this chapter of the journey.

Have you been blindsided by a major change you didn't want or anticipate? Can you flip the event from a negative (a lost opportunity) into a positive (an opportunity gained)?

If your schedule suddenly opened up, what is something you'd like to explore doing? Or is there something you've always wanted to do but haven't yet given yourself permission?


What are the first steps you can take to see if you can make your goal happen?

# 為せば成る

*(Naseba naru.)*

If you aim to accomplish
something, you can do it.

# 16 Journey to a New Land

It was still dark when Mom and Dad pulled up in front of Eva's house. On this cold January morning, they were taking me to the airport. In a few hours, I would be on a plane flying to Oakland, California.

We talked all the way to Denver International Airport. We talked about how I was doing with the separation. We talked about what my experience might be like in California. What was I most looking forward to? Was there anything I was worried about?

I shared how excited – and nervous – I was. I would be meeting Hendricks Sensei, who'd been my role model since I started Aikido two years earlier. She was an amazing martial artist, so strong, so powerful. And not strong and powerful "for a woman," but as a martial artist, period.

I described what I'd seen on YouTube of her doing a demonstration with live swords. Her skill and precision in throwing armed Ukes left me in awe. And soon, I would be meeting her.

We talked about their upcoming trips. Dad was a private pilot and the two of them flew often in their Cessna 182. They were getting close to their goal of landing in every state, and in June, they'd be taking another long trip flying to Alaska.

I missed my parents so much and wished I'd been living with them instead of Eva, but I just didn't feel it was safe to do that. They'd come over to Eva's a few times for dinner, and I'd go see them when I could, but not nearly as much as I would have liked.

Dad pulled up to the curb and we all got out of his silver Volvo. He pulled my carry-on bag and long red Aikido weapons bag out of the trunk and put them on the sidewalk. Inside my weapons bag were my wooden bokken (sword), jo (staff), and tanto (knife). Hendricks Sensei was an expert in Aikido weapons, and training in them was an integral part of her dojo.

The three of us hugged so hard and I started crying.

"I love you so much." I wiped away the tears with the sleeve of my coat. "I'll call you when I get to the dojo."

"We're so proud of you, honey," said Mom. Dad nodded. Both of their eyes were glistening.

My journey to be Uchi Deshi for Patricia Hendricks Sensei was about to begin. She'd devoted her life to Aikido and teaching, and had built a strong student base. Her dojo building was old and filled with history, including the story of Bruce Lee's family gathering there the night he died. It had living quarters for Uchi Deshi like me, so we could live, breathe, and support the dojo 24/7.

I was about to step out of the life I knew and into a life I didn't, and while I'd tried to be as prepared as possible, I had no idea what lay ahead.

When I landed at the Oakland airport, I headed to the baggage carousel to get my weapons bag. As I looked for the oversize luggage area to find my red Bujin bag, I heard a voice behind me.

"Kara?"

I turned around. There was Hendricks Sensei and her son Connor.

On the plane, I'd reviewed the Uchi Deshi packet of instructions. I was ready to take the BART train from the airport to the dojo. The last thing I ever expected was for Hendricks Sensei to pick me up.

"Hendricks Sensei," I bowed. "What an honor to meet you. And this must be your son." I bowed to Connor as well.

I added, "I was going to take the BART, Sensei. I hope this is not a big inconvenience for you. And I so appreciate you being here." I hoped my nervousness wasn't too obvious, and I wasn't sure what to say or how to express my surprise and gratitude at being met at the airport by Hendricks Sensei.

"It's my pleasure," she said. "When I heard the time you'd be landing, I knew I wanted to pick you up. It's really special to have a woman come be Uchi Deshi and Blevins Sensei has shared what a serious student you are."

Connor took my weapons bag (even though I tried not to let him carry it) and we made our way outside into the bright California sun. It might have been cold in Colorado when I left that morning, but the Bay Area was about 60 degrees.

On the way to the dojo, Sensei asked about my training, how I got into Aikido, what my goals were, and other things.

A few miles later, she said, "There aren't any classes this afternoon at the dojo, so I thought we'd stop on the way for a little break."

We took an exit and ended up on a cute little side street with shops and a park across the street. "Connor loves basketball, and I said we could play a bit after we picked you up."

With Connor and Hendricks Sensei giving me tips, we played a little two-on-one and a game of Horse. It was neck and neck between Hendricks Sensei and Connor for most of the match. I wasn't even in the running.

Between hearing the ball swoosh through the net and the thump of dribbling, I kept mentally pinching myself.

Here I am… playing basketball with Hendricks Sensei and her son. This is so surreal. And I am so grateful to be here.

We wrapped up our game and walked to the coffee shop. I tried to buy a coffee for Hendricks Sensei but she insisted on treating me.

We sipped our way back to the car and arrived at the dojo a few minutes later.

Aikido of San Leandro was tucked into a small block of businesses on MacArthur Street. The green awning and the trees in planters flanking the dojo door gave it a very warm, welcome feeling. Behind the dojo was a quiet neighborhood of classic California bungalows.

It was late afternoon when we arrived. Here was my home for the next seven days.

Hendricks Sensei and Connor helped me get settled. My room would be the Uchi Deshi quarters reached by a ladder above the women's changing room. Its shoji screen window opened over the dojo. With a low ceiling and space for my gi and non-Aikido clothing in a cabinet at the end of the futon, it also had a reading lamp and a meditation altar with candles and incense from previous Uchi Deshi.

Downstairs, the kitchen and two bathrooms (one with a shower) were at the back of the dojo. Off the kitchen, Hendricks Sensei's small office had a narrow stairway to her personal meditation space and sleeping area. The men's changing room was across the hall from the women's, both just a few feet through a doorway that led to the dojo.

The first thing I'd noticed when I bowed in to the dojo a few minutes before was the palpable energy of the place. Stepping into the dojo was like stepping into a portal. It was filled with peace and vibrance and safety and wisdom and strength and connection to the universe.

A few minutes before sunset, Hendricks Sensei explained that she did a fire ceremony twice a day at the dojo. She said I was welcomed to sit behind her on the mat and observe.

I kneeled in seiza and she began. First she started the song Om Namah Shivaya on the computer in the front office. Then, bowing in, she lit dung in the fire box and began saying the prayers that joined the sweet tendrils of smoke climbing into the air above the Shomen.

In the last of the day's light, I held open the front dojo door for Sensei and carried her purse out to the car. Standing at the end of the sidewalk, I bowed and watched until I could no longer see her car as it turned the corner.

I turned around and entered the dojo, bowing, then softly locked the door behind me. My Uchi Deshi experience had begun.

After I got settled and made myself dinner from the protein bars and orange in my purse, I read and re-read my instructions and all the notices on the dojo walls. I wanted to be as prepared as I could for the next morning, when my alarm would chime at 5:15 to get the dojo ready for 6:00 class.

Before climbing the ladder one last time to go to sleep in my living quarters, I bowed onto the mat and bowed to the Shomen. I sat for a while on the firm, cool canvas, surrounded by the peace of the dojo with soft lights illuminating the space.

In this coming week, I prayed, let me be open, quiet, and grateful for the learning and the people I have the honor of serving.

**Your Turn**: You may want to take a bit of time to answer the following questions. They may help you capture and explore your own thoughts as they relate to the concepts from this chapter of the journey.

Do you have a dream of doing something way outside your comfort zone, something that will take a great deal of commitment and may even be scary? What is it?

As you contemplate doing it, what are you feeling?

Is there a teacher you'd love to learn from? Who is that and why?

Who can help you put your dream into action?

How can you prepare for the experience?

# 一点一画もおろそかにしない

*(Itten ikkaku mo orosoka ni shinai.)*

# Don't neglect the slightest of details.

# 17 Opening to the Unknown

For the next seven days, I awoke at 5:15 and climbed down the ladder from my sleeping quarters. I put the kettle on, then bowed into the dojo. My day started with vacuuming and straightening the front of the dojo where students placed their shoes when they entered. I tidied the front office and cued up Sensei's fire ceremony song. Later that morning after class, she shared how to take care of the ceremony area and what needed to be done to prepare it for the evening ceremony.

Next, I dusted the Shomen, carefully lifting up each item, one at a time, to dust it and underneath it, making my way down the length of the Shomen. Next, I did the same with the items under the Shomen. If any of the flowers in the vases were wilting, I'd remove them. Stepping back and carefully looking at the Shomen, I made sure that it was clean, orderly, and pleasing to the eye.

I had a cup of coffee and a small breakfast and then cleaned up my dishes. I put the kettle on again, and pre-prepared a cup of tea and piece of fruit and maybe some nuts for Sensei, which would be waiting on her desk after the fire ceremony.

I made sure the bathrooms were clean and changed into my gi.

A few minutes before Sensei would arrive for the morning fire ceremony, I'd unlock the front door, put the sign out on the sidewalk, sweep the sidewalk and doorway, and be ready to meet Sensei at the curb when she arrived. Carrying her purse and opening the door, I started the song and Sensei did the fire ceremony.

Morning class was typically quiet and the overhead lights were left off. Students entered the dojo, bowed onto the mat, changed into their gi, and sat in seiza. After class, there was a bit more talking as students were off to work or wherever their day took them.

After everyone left, I vacuumed the front of the dojo and office again, tidied the Shomen, and dusted the other areas of the dojo that I hadn't earlier. I took time in the morning to practice my weapons or rolls on the firm mats or shadow practice of Aikido techniques using an imaginary partner.

After that, I changed out of my gi to walk to the little neighborhood market a few blocks away. I bought fresh fruit, greens, nuts, protein, yogurt. Back at the dojo, I made lunch and sat outside on the little walkway overlooking the alley. It was usually sunny and quiet, and I'd enjoy a few minutes of down time.

The first class of the afternoon was the kids class at 5:00, followed by adult class at 6:00. After my lunch, I had a few hours to do administrative tasks or dojo projects that I'd noticed and thought would be helpful.

One day, Sensei asked me to pick up the new dojo flyers from the print shop several miles away. I rode the very tall dojo bike to get them, leaning it way over at every stop sign so my foot

could straddle the frame and touch the ground. On other days, I organized the kitchen cabinets, sorted kitchen tools and cookware, deep cleaned the spice rack, cleaned and organized the refrigerator and the drawer of dry food, cereal, pasta, and crackers.

Later in the week, I loaded the dojo laundry into a big plastic bag and walked to the laundromat a couple miles away. Washed, dried, and folded, I carried it back and put it neatly into the dressers in the men's and women's locker rooms.

If there were any voice messages on the dojo answering machine, I called them back if it was a simple request for information on classes, or I took a message and left it on Sensei's desk for her to return the call later.

And so the afternoons unfolded during my stay as Uchi Deshi.

About an hour before the kids class, I started preparing. I made sure the Shomen was orderly, prepped the fire box and music for the afternoon ceremony, pre-prepared tea and a snack for Hendricks Sensei, cleaned the front of the dojo, checked the bathrooms, changed into my gi, and met Hendricks Sensei as she pulled up outside the front door.

After class ended and everyone had gone home, I was once again in the quiet, nurturing space of the dojo. Only the soft lights above the Shomen lit the space. I made my rounds to be sure things were ready for morning class. Then I sat in front of the Shomen, giving thanks for the day and my learning and the people on my path.

At 10:30, I climbed the ladder to my room and turned off the light. Another day as Uchi Deshi complete.

I expected the hard training of being Uchi Deshi. Three hours of class every day, and often being Sensei's Uke. Extra practice on my own. Kneeling in seiza over and over. Taking hundreds of falls every day. The normal bumps and bruises of Aikido. By the third day, my knees were aching and stiff, voicing their opinion on sitting in seiza so much when they were used to just four hours in a whole week. My left foot resembled a flipper after I twisted it during ukemi. One night as I was climbing down the ladder to go to the bathroom, I missed the bottom rung and crashed to the floor. No broken bones, just a bruised backside. And none of this was a big enough issue that an ice pack, Arnica, and ibuprofen couldn't fix.

What I didn't expect was the heart-opening gratitude it filled me with, along with the deep realization that service is the highest honor. I found joy in helping Sensei, keeping the dojo clean, noticing small things I could do in my afternoons to keep the dojo running smoothly.

I was humbled by the kindness given to me by so many students, and their guidance was priceless.

During our classes at Kiryu Aikido, Sensei had taught me to watch what my Sempai were doing. Because of their time in the dojo, they would show by their actions what needed to be done and what was expected. My Sempai at Aikido of San Leandro did that as well.

Hendricks Sensei took time with me and shared her deep wisdom, experiences of training so closely with Morihiro Saito Sensei, and her understanding of life on many levels. She invited me to dinner at her house, and one evening we went to Berkely to window shop and have an ice cream. I will always remember her generosity, kindness, and wisdom.

The other thing I was surprised – and grateful – to discover was the deep, deep peace I found within myself. Essentially spending a week in silent meditation and service had reset something in me. Finally, I felt like the quiet on the outside was joined by the quiet on the inside.

**Your Turn**: You may want to take a bit of time to answer the following questions. They may help you capture and explore your own thoughts as they relate to the concepts from this chapter of the journey.

As you begin the new experience you've been planning, what if it goes very differently than you expect?

What if you can let go of the outcome or any goals you have associated with this, and just be present in the experience and wherever it goes?

Are you ready for the possibility of letting change happen?

# 虎穴に入らずんば虎子を得ず

*(Koketsu ni irazumba koji o ezu.)*

You cannot catch a tiger cub unless you enter the tiger's den.

# 18 Facing the Mirror

When my parents picked me up at the airport a week later, I'm sure I looked the same on the outside. But I felt very, very different on the inside. I noticed things, I saw more details, I listened more deeply, to what was going on around me and what was going on within me.

One of those things was that I was ready to move out of hiding and start living in the world again. Whatever happened, I was ready to risk it.

Mary stopped in at Eva's one afternoon in early February. Her Mom had decided to move out of the cute little house they'd built for her on Mary's property. She wanted to move into town to be closer to her friends at the senior center.

"Her house will be available in a week or two," Mary said. "Are you interested?"

Eva said I was welcome to stay as long as I needed to. I also didn't want to be a burden and impose. She'd been so kind and generous.

Moving to Mary's seemed like the perfect next step. Eva would have her guest room back but I'd still stop by often and help with her horses when she needed a hand. My horses would move into the front corral at Mary's and have their own shed and small pasture. I'd actually be able to see them from my new kitchen window.

The issue I had to face was moving back to the neighborhood where John still lived. The raw edges of leaving John had softened and started to mend. I was no longer in fear for my life, and John and I had met a few times in safe, public places. I wouldn't be going back, that was clear. But we could talk like human beings and share thoughts and feelings. That was a first.

John and I met for coffee, and I shared that I'd be moving to Mary's. Even though he never knew where I'd gone when I moved out, he thought that moving to Mary's would be good for the horses and me. He also agreed to ground rules about not driving up Mary's road and not stopping by.

I moved myself, Eddie, and Serena to Mary's a few weeks after getting back from San Leandro. The rhythm of Practice settled in again, as days of Practice turned into weeks, then months.

As winter melted into the green of spring, Sensei said that our dojo would be testing again in a few months. For those who were ready, our tests would take place as part of a seminar with several guest instructors and dojos participating. This meant there would be quite a crowd to watch the tests.

Sensei also said that he was recommending me to test for Ikkyu – the last brown belt rank before one reaches the black belt levels.

"Hai, Sensei," I said, and bowed deeply. I knew I had a lot of work ahead of me to be ready.

I asked my Sempai Les-san to be Uke for my Ikkyu test, and I asked if he and John-san would help me prepare. They both kindly and

generously agreed, and we spent many hours in extra practice sessions over the next several weeks.

Finally, the day of the seminar and testing arrived. It was fun having so many students on the mat and I did my best to pick up the nuances of the guest instructors' different styles. I was also glad to have the seminar before our tests. It was a great way to burn off some nervous energy and be fully warmed up.

When it was finally time for Les-san and me to bow in and begin my test in front of so many people, I was happy and ready for it. As we walked to the edge of the mat, I thought back to something Les-san had said many times during our extra practices. "In your test, slow down and show your technique. It isn't about speed; it's about clean, strong Aikido. Just do what we always practice."

The test was truly fun and I enjoyed the experience. At one point, Izawa Sensei asked for a certain technique and I did a different one, not out of disrespect but because of muscle memory. Many students revert to the techniques we like doing the most or are most comfortable with. Just as I was finishing the technique, I realized what I'd done. I smiled inside and once again heard the voice of Sensei in many classes saying, "If you make a mistake in a test, finish the technique strongly, then do the next one correctly."

I adjusted to do the next technique as requested and finished the test, feeling good about it. Les-san's ukemi was beautiful and of course made the test even better.

After the tests, normal Practice resumed at the dojo. I took the growth and learning I'd gained from preparing for and passing my Ikkyu test and used it to deepen my Practice even more, dedicating myself to learning and growing.

Several months later, during class one night, Sensei said that our dojo would be testing again with the other dojos. My next test would be for Shodan, first-degree black belt. Would I be ready?

Over the coming months, I worked hard. Harder than I ever had. Once again, I reached out to my Sempai Les-san and John-san for their help. Both said yes.

I worked with them on my open hand techniques and Jo Dori, Tachi Dori, and Tanto Dori, where Uke would attack with a weapon and I'd move in with a technique with the outcome being to neutralize the attack with a takeaway, a pin, a throw, or a combination. We also practiced Koshi Nage – hip throws – where I'd load them over my back and throw in a big arc using my hips as the pivot point.

I worked on my Jiyu Waza, both after class with partners and shadow practice in the garage at Mary's with an invisible partner. For this part of the test, I'd be doing a series of techniques from different attacks by one Uke. Not scripted or choreographed, Jiyu Waza was a flow of techniques showing my understanding and ability to execute each cleanly, with power, and with the continual awareness of Zanshin linking them all together. In my garage shadow practice, I moved through the techniques with flow, feeling and envisioning my Uke attacking. Feeling the timing and placement of my footwork. Opening. Entering. Tenkan. Irimi.

Jiyu Waza was different from Randori, though. The Randori part of my test would have multiple attackers and the goal was staying calm, centered, not getting trapped at the edge of the mat, staying aware of where attackers were, and dealing with each attack in a technique or an intentional deflection.

Normal Practice continued, too.

One night after we bowed out and thanked our partners, Sensei asked to talk with me for a few minutes. We stepped outside the dojo into the cool evening air and I relished the breeze through my sweat-soaked gi.

I expected him to say something along the lines of how hard I was practicing, how much I was improving, and to keep up the hard work until my Shodan test.

"Your techniques are looking really solid," he began. "And it's great how you're working with your Sempai to get in extra practice."

"Thank you," I said. "I'm so grateful for Les-san and John-san's help. I couldn't do this without them."

"That's the great part of a strong dojo like ours," he said, then paused. "So like I said, your techniques are ready for Shodan," he said.

I bowed slightly in thanks. "But your martial spirit is not there yet. Your spirit has a long way to go to be at the Shodan level."

He paused. "You might not be ready to test in the fall. Keep practicing and we'll see."

I was stunned. Absolutely stunned. This was not the conversation I expected. Not at all.

I thought I was doing a great job preparing. Pushing myself out of my comfort zone. Practicing at a higher level. I envisioned me on the mat and saw this big presence, full of calm confidence and power.

"Hai, Sensei," I said. I knew the answer in the dojo is "hai."

Hai means yes. I understand. I hear the instruction. I'm listening.

Hai was all I could say, and even if it was appropriate for me to share more (which it wasn't), I couldn't. I was in shock. Deep shock.

As I drove home, my emotions spilled out.

"Martial spirit?!," I yelled to my steering wheel. "What do you mean I don't have martial spirit?! Watch, I'll show you martial spirit!"

I was angry and embarrassed and in shock, and then angry again, and then frustrated. Then the tears of shame and unworthiness streamed down my face.

What the heck was he talking about? I'd just come through the biggest, hardest – and truly life-threatening – challenge of my life. And I made it through. If that's not martial spirit, I don't know what is, I thought to myself.

This emotion was countered by my feelings that I'd never be good at Aikido. I was short, female, older, I didn't learn fast, and I started way too late. Who was I kidding… thinking I could be a martial artist?

When I got home, I went out to see my horses. Eddie and Serena were always such good listeners and counselors. As they munched a flake of hay, I sat in the corner of the barn and slowed my breathing and let my body and brain calm down.

Ok, I thought to myself. What just happened, and why do I feel completely blindsided? Is there truth to what Sensei said? Could he be right?

I wrestled with the disconnect. How can I feel this enormous presence and spirit on the inside of me... but he doesn't see it on the outside?

As I sat there, soothed by the rhythmic chewing of my dear horses, I saw that I had a choice. The conversation earlier that evening had brought me squarely to a fork in the road.

One road: accept the fact that I didn't have the martial spirit I needed to have to test for Shodan right now. Work harder and dig deeper and let that spirit start to grow so it would show on the outside.

Another road: accept that this was all I had in me. If it wasn't good enough, I didn't have any more to give. I'd never be the martial artist I wanted to be, and I might as well quit.

Which road would I take?

I could take an honest look at my Practice, and accept that I could work even harder and commit to allowing my spirit to find its way out.

I could let my demoralized ego take control of my future, saying this isn't fair, I tried my best and it isn't good enough. I'll never be good enough, so why even try.

I stood up and gave Eddie and Serena both a hug. Their soft, strong, warm necks held me.

**Your Turn**: You may want to take a bit of time to answer the following questions. They may help you capture and explore your own thoughts as they relate to the concepts from this chapter of the journey.

Are you facing a disconnect between what you imagine yourself to be and what the world sees?

What is a way you can take a step back and look at the situation?

Can you see how criticism or feedback can either spur you to action to make true, deep change… or keep you rooted in what you know and what's comfortable?

Does the information shared have a piece of truth to it? If so, how can you use it to help you grow and become even better?

Is the feedback from someone who doesn't want to see you succeed, who wants to hold you back? There are those people in life. There are also those who shine the harsh light of truth to help you grow into what they know you can become.

# 心焉に在らざれば、視れども見えず

*(Kokoro koko ni arazareba, miredomo miezu.)*

If a person is there in body but not in spirit, they will look without seeing.

# 19 Perseverance

At the next class, I bowed onto the mat, quieting my mind and the inner chatter in preparation for the class ahead. I was here for one reason: to focus on my Practice. To Practice hard and well, letting go of how much I thought I knew, letting go of "proving," letting go of pushing. Just allowing in the learning.

Every time my mind got busy, I used it as a reminder to focus back into class.

One movement, one fall, one throw, one bow, one technique. The class continued, a flow of moments, and in each one, I did my best to stay present.

At the end of class, I was still winded, my gi was still drenched in sweat, I was still exhilarated at the physicality of a hard class. But I noticed a difference: a quietness in me. I couldn't explain it, but I could feel it.

The next class, I bowed in with the same intention: focus simply on my Practice. Plus, in this class I began to explore my martial spirit.

Some might think that martial spirit is aggression, outward displays of dominance over your partner, or loud kiai. Essentially, frothing at the mouth and screaming, eyes wide and unblinking, focused on the battle ahead.

But to me, that was not martial spirit, that was anger, rage, or bloodlust. It might be needed on the battlefield in hand-to-hand combat in World War I. But to my battlefield, here on the mat, I wanted to bring something different.

I envisioned my martial spirit as a presence: big, unwavering, focused energy that continued from the time I bowed onto the mat until I bowed off.

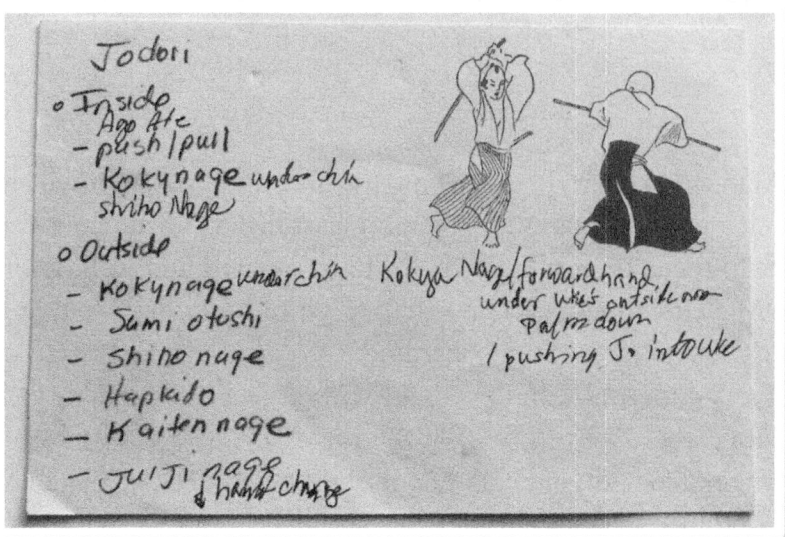

I envisioned owning the mat. Owning my technique. Owning my space. Owning my focus before, during, and after each technique, both as Uke and Nage.

I could not change being a 5-foot-tall 44-year-old woman, but I could change my presence on the mat.

I started to kiai with more intention and intensity. O-Sensei used these loud vocalizations to unbalance opponents. After I threw my partner, I maintained my Zanshin (awareness) of the situation and was ready when they got up. I invited their next attack. Come on. Sakoi – let's go.

I Practiced with more focus than I ever had. And over the next few classes, I realized how much more I had in me that I hadn't tapped yet. I thought I'd been practicing to my fullest, but now I saw I was holding back. Reserving energy for… I wasn't sure what.

As the weeks passed, I was changing. This deeper focus was no longer something I had to think about and remind myself to do. It was becoming me. The way I Practiced. The energy and presence I brought to the mat.

The test date was now less than a month away. In class one night after we'd practiced for an hour, Sensei called Yame. We all lined up at the edge of the mat.

"We're going to do some Randori practice to finish the class," he said. "Ukes, attack with Yokomen. Remember, even though this is Randori, I still want to see full, clean techniques." He added, "I want to see you're aware of where your attackers are. Use the space. Don't get trapped in a corner."

Les-san went first. We attacked with Yokomen strikes to the side of his head. Les-san responded with Kotegaeshi. Sumi Otoshi. Irimi Nage. Clean techniques. Moving on to the next attack with awareness and flow.

"Yame!" Sensei called out.

Les-san and Ukes kneeled, bowing in thanks.

When it was my turn, my Ukes lined up facing me in the middle of the mat.

I bowed and called out "Hajime!" Begin!

They came at me with strong Yokomen attacks. I responded with Irimi Nage, Kokyu Nage, Kotegaeshi, Shiho Nage. When I was in danger of getting trapped in the crowd of attackers, I slipped through an opening and stepped to another place on the mat. If they paused in their attack, I moved to them.

Time and space blended. Attacks and techniques blended. I was no longer being attacked and then deciding to do a technique. I was in the energy. Techniques flowed, tied to the attack, not separate from it. I invited them in. As O-Sensei said, "Invite them in, then send them on their way."

"Yame!"

I stopped. Ukes stopped. We faced each other, kneeled in seiza, bowed, and went back to the line of students at the edge of the mat.

Other students took their turns in the center for Randori practice. Attackers, techniques, moving, flowing.

On the drive home, I mentally reviewed the Randori. I realized for the first time, I had stayed centered. I didn't get trapped. It's almost like I anticipated Uke's attack and moved to it, rather than being one second late. And the biggest thing? I wasn't exhausted.

Sometimes, practicing with multiple attackers would become an anaerobic workout – not breathing during the techniques and having no oxygen left at the end. Afterwards, I'd always felt like I'd sprinted the quarter mile. Tonight, though, felt completely different – like an exchange of movement – and the entire time, I was breathing. I was aware. I was calm.

The next class, I again simply focused on my Practice. With intention, awareness, presence. It was my new way of being, and I kept exploring how deep I could go.

I'd let go the importance of testing for Shodan. It was no longer a big deal. Either I would be recommended to test or I wouldn't.

If I tested, I might pass or I might fail. Either way, my Practice would continue.

After class that night, Sensei asked to talk with me.

"You've really come a long way, Kara-san," he said. "Your Zanshin and martial spirit are much stronger. Keep working on it. I think you may be ready to test."

---

**Your Turn**: You may want to take a bit of time to answer the following questions. They may help you capture and explore your own thoughts as they relate to the concepts from this chapter of the journey.

What's a turning point or a fork in the road you're facing? What direction will you choose?

Where is there an opportunity to explore letting go of the outcome? What would it feel like if you focused on the process and the energy you bring to the activity instead of the end result?

Is there an area where you can make the decision to dig deeper than you ever have? A place you can explore the possibility that there is more within you... waiting to be tapped?

# 備えあれば
# 憂いなし

*(Sonae areba urei nashi.)*

If you prepare, nothing
will cause you distress.

# 20 Welcome to My Mat

The morning of my Shodan test dawned cool and clear. I walked to the barn to feed Eddie and Serena and sat with them a while with my coffee. As my hands curled around the warm mug and the steam swirled into the chilly November air, I thought back on the path that had brought me here.

Not just here with my beloved horses, which was time I cherished. But also Here – living in Mary's little house, living in the liminal space between what had been and what was ahead.

Life as I had known it had been upended, the future was uncertain, and yet amid all the external swirling, I felt grounded. I felt more centered than I ever remembered. I knew that whatever happened – in my black belt test in a few hours or in my life in the next months and years – I could handle it.

I met Les-san in Castle Rock, and then we picked up Sensei at his house. We piled our weapons cases and gi bags into Les-san's car and started on the hour-long drive to Louisville.

As Les-san and Sensei talked about various things in the front seat, I visualized my test while I imagined the butterflies in my belly flying a gentle, rhythmic pattern timed with my breath. I wasn't worried about my test, but I was definitely thinking about it.

I felt the movements and focus as I visualized starting the test with Suwari Waza techniques from a kneeling position. Move in and bring up my inside knee as I blend with Uke's strike. Knee walk – no shuffling – in to do Ikkyo, Nikyo, Sankyo, Yonko, both Omote (front) and Ura (behind) versions. Then Hanmi Handachi – where I'm kneeling and my Uke attacks from standing.

Next, I run through all the variations I can think of for each attack that Sensei will call out.

I especially envision my Koshi Nage section, where I'll throw Les-san with hip throws. I enter in and throw with 100% energy and focus. In Koshi Nage, throws have to be committed and strong. Otherwise, it's not Aikido, and it's not safe. I've seen many tests where the Uke just lays across Nage's hip and rolls off. There's no throw, no energy, no commitment. That's not what I will bring to my test.

Next, I visualize my Jiyu Waza segment. For my black belt test, Uke will attack from Shomen Uchi and I review each of the techniques that flow well from this attack to my head. I flow, I blend with Uke's energy and direction. My footwork is precise. I move with Ki Ken Tai Ichi – my body and spirit are one.

Then I visualize Randori – multiple attackers. I see the openings and move in. I invite my Ukes to attack with "come on, come get me" energy. I flow from technique to technique, staying present and super aware of where my Ukes are. When I'm in danger of getting trapped in the middle of the mob, I slip through an opening and let them come to me. I move around the mat, using the space.

With my visualized test finished and strong, I come back to listening to the conversation. I'm not hungry at all, but I know I'll need energy for my test. And I also know that my test will be later in the morning, after the kids' tests and the lower kyu adult tests.

"If you're hungry, here are some protein bars," as I hand two to the front seat for Sensei and Les-san. They unwrap their bars and I do the same. I choke down the bar with swallows of water. This brought back memories of eating a bagel and peanut butter at 5:00 in the morning, walking to the glow of my headlamp, when John and I would start hiking the approach to climbing a Fourteener. It took us 15 years, but we climbed all the peaks over 14,000 feet in Colorado.

Those days seem long, long ago.

We pulled into the parking lot and waved to familiar faces. The tests were at Izawa Sensei's Tanshinjuku dojo, which used the space in a childcare facility with a gymnastics room. It had a spring floor, bright blue with fabric that felt like the outside of a tennis ball. Taking ukemi on this floor was a joy.

Students and families from three dojos began to arrive. While we all practiced different styles of Aikido, we tested together under Kei and Mariquita Izawa Sensei. Getting together with our Aikido community was something I always looked forward to.

Sensei, Les-san, and I bowed in to the gym and helped the Tanshinjuku students prepare the space for testing. We moved the big crash pad mats out of the way, stacking them so visitors could sit on them like bleachers. We vacuumed the mat and helped set up the Shomen.

Finally, it was time to get dressed. Testing would start in 15 minutes.

Lining up in seiza alongside Les-san and other students of varying ranks, we all bowed in.

Onegaishimasu.

Izawa Sensei welcomed us all and shared his philosophy of testing. It was not to show sheer strength and dominating our Ukes with physical power.

It was to share our Aikido and what we have been practicing. To show our flow and martial spirit. Our techniques and resilience. To be proud of our Practice and share the joy of it with others.

With that, testing started with the youngest students: two sisters of about 5 and 6 years old.

I watched each test and watched my breathing. Staying centered.

Finally, it was my turn.

"Kara-san and Uke for Shodan," called Sensei.

Les-san and I stood up and walked to opposite edges of the mat, then turned toward the Shomen and walked up the edge to the center of the space.

"Welcome to my mat," I said silently to myself, to O-Sensei, to Les-san, to the students who would be my Ukes for Randori. "I'm glad to share this time with you."

At the edge of the mat, we turned in unison and bowed to each other, then stepped on to the mat and walked to meet in the center. We

turned to face the Shomen, then kneeled into seiza together.

"Shomen ni rei," I said, as we both bowed to the Shomen.

"Sensei ni rei," as we bowed to the Senseis.

"Ota gai ni rei," as we turned toward each other and bowed.

Sensei called out my first techniques. "Suwari Waza, Ikkyo through Yonko." Kneeling attacks and techniques.

Les-san raised his hand to strike to my head while moving in. I blended with his attack and took it into Ikkyo. First Omote, then Ura.

After the first attack, I initiated the strike.

Next Sensei called "Tachi Waza." These were my standing techniques.

By the time a student tests for Shodan, Sensei no longer called out specific techniques. Instead, he called out the attack that Uke would use, and then Nage would do 6-8 techniques from the attack.

First, he called for Shomen Uchi, a strike to the center of the head. I countered with Irimi Nage, Kotegaeshi, Ikkyo, Kokyu Nage, Sumi Otoshi, then blending to the inside for Nikyo Ura and the pin.

Next, he called for Yokomen Uchi, side strike to the head. Next, Morote Dori, two hands on one. Then Katate Dori, one hand grab. Ryote Dori, grabbing both hands. Ushiro Ryote Dori, grabbing both hands from the back.

Les-san attacked, over and over, and I flowed into the techniques.

Finally it was time for Koshi Nage, doing several hip throw techniques, I loaded him on my lower back for a second before using a circular movement and centrifugal energy to throw him.

"Hai, Yame," Sensei called. "Seiza."

Les-san and I kneeled on the mat facing each other. This was an opportunity for both of us to breathe, slow our heart rate, and settle for a few moments.

Next, it was time for weapons techniques. Les-san picked up the Tanto (wooden knife) and bowed to the Shomen. He attacked first with Tsuki, a strike to the abdomen. I responded with Kotegaeshi, Sankyo, Irimi Nage and others.

Then Yokomen attacks to the side of my head. Gokkyo, Tenbin Nage, Kotegaeshi ending with a pin and knife takeaway.

As we'd practiced so many times in the dojo, I didn't give the weapon back to Les-san. I put it on the mat, safely out of reach so he had to get it and I controlled where he was. We are what we Practice… and if we Practice giving a captured weapon back to our attacker, we train ourselves to do that on the street.

Les-san bowed off with the Tanto and picked up the Jo (wooden staff) for Jo Dori. He bowed toward the Shomen and toward me. Then he attacked with a strong, straight Tsuki to my chest. I moved inside, then outside, varying the techniques and throws. Ago Ate, Juji Nage, Hakkyo, Kokyu Nage.

Next was Tachi Dori – attacks with the Bokken (wooden sword). Les-san came at me with intention and power in a strong Menuchi strike to my head. I entered to the outside. Irimi Nage, Kokyu Nage, Kotegaeshi. I entered to the inside. Ago Ate, Sankyo, Kokyu Nage.

"Hai, Yame. Seiza."

Les-san and I took a few deep, slow breaths.

"Hai. Jiyu Waza. Uke attack with Yokomen Uchi."

"Welcome to my mat," I said again to myself.

The freestyle segment of my test was the opportunity to show clear technique, presence, flow, and calmness, as well as ownership of each movement. Precise footwork and hand movement, not muddy, not rushing. Finish each technique with Zanshin and flow into the next technique.

Own the mat. Use the space to your advantage. Move around the mat so Uke has to come to you.

Over the years, I'd seen Sensei's uncanny ability to know just when to call "Yame" during a test. It was always just before Nage ran out of techniques and started repeating.

"Hai, Yame," he called. "Seiza."

Les-san kneeled at one edge of the mat and I kneeled at the other. We took a few breaths as John-san and Keith-san bowed on to the mat and lined up with Les-San. It was time for Randori.

"Take a minute," said Sensei, "and start when you're ready."

After a few deep breaths, I bowed and called out "Hajime!"

I jumped to my feet and ran toward my Ukes. They moved in with strong attacks – Tsuki, Shomen Uchi, Yokomen Uchi. I entered in, responding with a technique, flowing from one to the next. If I was in danger of getting trapped, I slipped through an opening, or I blended past their attack to enter a safe place.

I did my best to own the mat, to stay aware of everyone's place, and to use a variety of techniques instead of defaulting to one. If my Ukes were holding back, I gave a loud kiai and moved toward them. "Sakoi!" is the term we use in the dojo. "Come get me!" I don't say it out loud, but I send out that energy with confidence and joy.

The blur of bodies attacking, moving, falling, standing up, attacking. The circular energy between us and surrounding us from each throw. Our connections created cursive strokes across the mat.

"Hai, Yame."

I finished my last throw and we returned in seiza to our original places on the mat. Through the deep breaths of catching our breath, I couldn't help it. A tiny smile emerged, and my Ukes smiled back.

"Ota gai ni rei," I called out, as we all bowed toward each other.

In unison, we turned slightly to the Senseis.

"Sensei ni rei," and we bowed.

Then we all faced forward to O-Sensei. "Shomen ni rei."

My Shodan test was complete.

**Your Turn**: You may want to take a bit of time to answer the following questions. They may help you capture and explore your own thoughts as they relate to the concepts from this chapter of the journey.

Are you preparing for a test or achievement that's outside your comfort zone, something you've never done before, or that you want to perform at a new level? Maybe it's your first 5K, 10K, or marathon, speaking in front of a large audience, singing at open-mic night, reading your poetry, taking the college entrance exam.

As you think about the situation or activity, is there anything you're worried about? What does it feel like?

Imagine bringing the feeling of "welcome to my mat" to both your Practice leading up to the event and the actual event. How does that change your energy about the situation? How can this help you?

What steps of your preparation and actual event can you visualize having the flow and ease you want to bring?

Prepare well, even over-prepare so you have the confidence you've put in the hours and hard work. On the day of the event, bow in mentally. Do what you've been practicing. Let go of the outcome. Whatever the scenario is, you can own the mat and welcome others to participate in the experience with you.

# 学問に近道なし

*(Gakumon ni chikamichi nashi.)*

There is no shortcut to scholarship.

# 21 Continuing on the Path

As I finished the test and bowed out, I realized something.

A Shodan test is a snapshot of where a student is on the path for that day and in that moment. The test pulls back the layers and shows what the student truly knows and has been learning. The test probably won't be perfect; there will be things that could have been done better. But the test will bring out what the student has been practicing all along.

As Sensei, Les-san, and Mark Rashid have shared with me many times, we are what we Practice. A test shows what we know, today. Raw, unfettered, exposed. If we've been practicing as hard as we can and as focused as we can, we will bring some of that to the test because it reflects how we've been practicing and the expectations of our teachers every class.

In contrast, if we've been practicing with sloppy techniques or lack of Zanshin, our hopes to improve that in a test probably won't happen. In my experience, it's not possible to bring in the "I WANT to bring X, Y, or Z to my test." We bring what we know and what is true for us. In my test, I would have loved to have brought huge round powerful elegant dynamic flowing movement to every bit of it. I daresay I didn't – and how exciting that I have all these things to work on for the next part of this journey.

I felt good about my test. I knew that my Practice was intense and focused to get there. I knew I gave it my all. I knew I had the best test possible I could have had on that day.

Was it perfect? No. And my Aikido's not perfect in the dojo. That's why I think it's great that the test captured where I am in my Aikido journey now. It showed some of the strengths and the many things I will be working on in the coming years. That is the beauty of

this. It's never over; the polishing and the growth never stop. That is an immense gift and one I'm so thankful for.

When all the tests were complete, Izawa Sensei and the other Senseis gathered in the corner of the dojo. They were discussing each test, how each student did, what they could improve, and whether they'd passed.

After a few minutes, they came to the center of the mat and faced the line of students. Senseis and students bowed, and we all sat in seiza.

"We have shared a great day of tests today," said Izawa Sensei. "As you have seen, we may have different styles and ways of doing techniques, but we all practice Aikido. For me, just as important as your technique is your martial spirit and respect for other students and dojos. That is why coming together as an Aikido community is so important."

Each Sensei took a few minutes to share a thought on the tests, on what had gone well and an idea to focus on for the future.

At the end, Izawa Sensei smiled. "We recommend all the students who tested today have passed and will be promoted to their next rank."

The following week, I bowed into the next Practice at the dojo.

At that moment, I started the next steps of this journey with my Sensei and Sempai and dojo. It was time to get back to work: back to Practice for the sake of Practice, back to Practicing for the joy of the journey.

I was also looking forward to repaying a tiny bit of the help given to me. Perhaps I could help others find the joy that results from the hard work, commitment, and dedication to their Practice.

It doesn't happen overnight, but class after class, day after day, year after year, I knew this with my whole being: Practice can lead to deep, positive change and grants the priceless opportunity to spend time with great people. I had seen this and experienced this so many times, and my Shodan test highlighted it yet again.

**Your Turn**: You may want to take a bit of time to answer the following questions. They may help you capture and explore your own thoughts as they relate to the concepts from this chapter of the journey.

After a big milestone or achievement, life can feel flat. You focused so long on the goal... and now it's over. What's ahead for you now? What's one way you can celebrate and honor your accomplishment, and then carry the momentum forward?

What are the lessons you learned from focusing on your goal?

What is the next goal or step you want to work toward?

How can you apply what you learned from your recent accomplishment to the next step of your journey?

*For black belt tests under the International Aikido Federation criteria, candidates are required to submit an essay about a topic relating to Aikido. The following is my Shodan test essay.*

### "A Shodan Test – Endings and Beginnings"

One of my favorite things in the fall is finding a deciduous tree with one branch turning yellow while the rest of the tree remains green. Or one leaf smolders orange amongst its still-green siblings.

To me, this signifies endings and beginnings in one simple, elegant statement. Where does summer end and fall begin? For a space in time, "endingsandbeginnings" are joined, becoming a singular thing.

On Saturday, November 7, 2009, I tested for my first degree black belt in Aikido. Known as "Shodan" – the first of the black belt ranks – it's an important step on the path of this martial art. And yet it's not really a step at all but an "endingandbeginning" – a natural and essential progression on this path, resulting from hard work, dedication, commitment, and help from one's teacher and dojo, and leading to more steps on this life-long journey that never ends. One season flows into the next, one year of Practice flows into the next. Leaf colors and belt colors may change, but the Practice and the process continue.

Many years ago, I heard it said that earning a black belt only means you're a serious student, nothing more. I may have first heard it from my horse teacher Mark Rashid, who also teaches Aikido. It's because of Mark that I started Aikido, and I thank him for bringing me to this path that is now an integral part of my life.

To many people, especially in America, a black belt seems to mean that you've attained the pinnacle of your martial arts achievement. The hard work is over. Now, to paraphrase Steve Martin from the movie *The Jerk*, "You are somebody!" Now you can coast a bit on the knowledge you've gained. Some people even quit after earning a black belt.

But really, the journey isn't over, it's just beginning. My teacher, Andrew Blevins Sensei, shared that in Japanese, "Sho" in Shodan means "beginner, beginning, fresh, new" – ah, not quite the pinnacle of achievement, now is it? :)

The more I train, the more I fully understand this notion. Only now do I understand some of the basics and can apply them more freely both on and off the mat. Only now, with some knowledge of the basics, can I start really learning about Aikido: we have to learn to walk before we can run. Only now is more of my Aikido being done from muscle memory and feel instead of thought and mental processing. I'm also starting to see that only now can I start to make my Aikido my own, based on my body type and approach.

Yes, I've worked hard to come to this place on the path. The process of being ready to test for Shodan didn't start a couple months ago; it started the first time I bowed in at Kiryu Aikido with Blevins Sensei. It took a lot of hard work, struggle, commitment, and focus from the very beginning. It took the enormous generosity of my Sensei and Sempai and fellow students over hundreds of days of Practice. Testing for Shodan was not my goal, but I knew it was a step I would need to commit to on this journey.

As Blevins Sensei shared with me a few tests ago, this is not an easy path, but the rewards are immeasurable if you choose to continue to push forward and do the hard work required. I think Aikido is the most difficult thing I've ever done. It hasn't come easily to me but I think I make up for it with determination, dedication, and sometimes stubborn commitment to persevering and keeping with it.

There have been a lot of challenges along the way; polishing off ego and smoothing off the rough edges from a human being are painful processes, and I've got a long way to go. And along with hard work there is indescribable joy and deep contentment. And huge life changes. Perhaps it's the hard work and the getting up one more time than we're thrown that makes the lessons so deep and profound.

Endingsandbeginnings. I look forward to getting to work and discovering what lies ahead.

# 時が解決する

*(Toki ga kaiketsu suru.)*

## Time brings resolution.

# 22 Leaning into Practice, Part I

As my Practice continued to build for the future, my marriage was coming to its conclusion.

Some people wondered why I hadn't filed for divorce immediately after I left. While I was in fear for my life, I also was in fear for John's.

His shock was deep when I left. He was moorless and adrift. I feared suicide was a very real solution for his pain.

At the same time, for the first time in our 23 years together, he showed remorse. He was sorry. He said he wanted to change.

I wanted to give him the gift of that possibility and the space to find out if he could discover life without rage being the only emotion he knew.

He attended anger management counseling. Many men in his group were court-ordered to be there. He didn't see his anger issues as being as bad as theirs. When the initial class was over, he said he'd done the work and had changed. No need to keep going to the class; he was done. Those other men might need to keep working on their anger, but he could handle his.

In the two years since I'd left, we'd also been to counseling. We'd even spent a little time together. Going for a hike, a movie, to dinner. Seeing if we could be a couple again.

But while the overt anger and light-switch rage weren't there, and for that I was thankful for John, I saw glimmers of what had always been. The anger simmering beneath the surface. I realized the trust – and therefore the love – had been broken many years before.

And I realized that expecting him to change his personality was not fair, just as it was not fair for him to expect me to change mine just to get along. I also wanted him to be free to find someone who could

love and appreciate him for the person he was, not the person I wanted him to be.

We met for coffee. This time, I wanted to share my heart in person, not a note left on a kitchen table because of fear. I told him that I deeply appreciated the work he'd done. I was glad he'd found a way to address his anger. I also shared that I knew I needed to move on with my life.

He wasn't happy with my decision. But he didn't explode and he didn't lash out. I was grateful. I honored the growth he'd done. And I was deeply sad.

It was a Friday afternoon when we met at the bank to sign the divorce papers. He signed his name so hard I thought the paper would tear under the pen. He couldn't talk about anger and loss. The pen did it for him.

In a few minutes, it was done. Twenty three years of hope, of dreams, of love during the good times, of what could be…. Done with the stroke of a pen and a stack of documents signed in triplicate.

That night at the dojo, I lined up with the other students.

Sensei bowed us in. As I bowed in return, the sharp sting of tears rose behind my eyes.

Through the warmups, I fought them back. It wouldn't be martial of me to cry in class.

A warrior doesn't cry. I channeled my feeling of loss and transformed it into energy for the class. Several times, the sting welled up. Somehow, I made it through class without the tears falling.

On the drive home, the tears were free. They rushed in with a torrent. Maybe warriors do cry.

*Real fearlessness is the product of tenderness. It comes from letting the world tickle your heart, your raw and beautiful heart. You are willing to open up, without resistance or shyness, and face the world. You are willing to share your heart with others.*

*To be a spiritual warrior, one must have a broken heart; without a broken heart and the sense of tenderness and vulnerability, your warriorship is untrustworthy.*

ChögyamTrungpa
Shambhala: The Sacred Path of the Warrior

**Your Turn**: You may want to take a bit of time to answer the following questions. They may help you capture and explore your own thoughts as they relate to the concepts from this chapter of the journey.

Are you facing a heartbreaking situation? What is it, and what does it feel like?

What have you done to come to a peaceful and positive solution?

Are you afraid of showing your tenderness?

What are some ways you can accept your tender heart with compassion and see your sadness as strength?

What is one way you can use your broken heart to feel more alive and bring that energy to good?

# なる様になる

*(Naru you ni naru.)*

# What will be will be.

# 23 A Door Opens

Practice continued. Life continued.

I moved out of Mary's guest house and into the house I'd bought in the same neighborhood. Eddie and Serena came home, and together we created our next stage of life.

In the dojo, I continued my Practice: to sweat, grow, get thrown, stand up, throw, and finish the technique with Zanshin.

My Nidan test came November 10, 2012. Working toward my second-degree black belt had a similar – but different – feel than my Shodan test. I knew what it was like to dig down and focus deeply. I'd also glimpsed from my Shodan test how deeply this journey could go.

I invited others in the dojo to be part of my test, and I was part of theirs that day. When my test was over, I was proud of it. I'd owned the mat and welcomed others to come join my test. I also felt my understanding getting stronger. But I also wondered. Would I ever feel my techniques were good enough?

These first six years of Aikido and the grounding of weekly Practice gave me strength and a sacred place to come. Practice centered me. It gave me a reason to get up on those dark mornings. It gave shape to my week. It gave me a strong, unmovable place to stand when all was swirling around me.

What I didn't know was how much more I would need Aikido in the years to come.

After the divorce, I continued to work as a proposal manager at a construction company. The unrelenting stress, the hours, the churn of creating and shipping proposal after proposal for large government contracts... the edges of life got smaller and smaller.

I knew it was killing me, or at the very least dimming my light to enjoy life, but I felt powerless to change. The loyalty and dedication I brought to my Practice and my dojo I also brought to the company and all my previous employers.

But instead of fulfilling me and making me stronger, it was slowly eroding who I was.

I knew it was time to quit; to do something that fed my soul instead of sucking it dry. But the depression and stress mired me there… until one Friday afternoon in late October 2013.

The company hadn't been winning the contracts it needed to, and on that day, several of my coworkers and I were told of the situation. We were being let go. It was a hard decision, blah blah blah blah, said the HR manager, the one whose crocodile smile on other occasions told the rest of us the depth of her true compassion. I don't remember all of what she said, and it didn't matter.

As I signed my severance papers, including the amusing statement that "I would not speak badly of the company or its management," the feeling I had was not sadness, anger, or confusion.

It was lightness. Relief. And joy. Pure joy. I was free. Released from my self-imposed prison.

While I would rather have left on my own terms, the relief of not having to come to work next week and crank out yet another proposal was huge.

As I packed up my office, I was humming. My boss noticed and commented that I didn't seem too upset that I'd just been laid off. She helped me carry my boxes down the stairwell and we chatted on the way out to my truck.

She was a good person, and I'd learned so much from her. One of the biggest things was "That's not my monkey," meaning don't take on other people's stress, negativity, and poor decision-making.

I gave her a big hug and thanked her for all she'd taught me. I climbed into my truck, closed the door, and smiled.

First, I called Mom and Dad with the news and how good I felt. I'd come up over the weekend for dinner.

When I got home, I sat with Eddie and Serena and shared the good news with them.

Then I texted Sensei.

Just a few days earlier, he'd boarded a plane to start a new job in California. This change had rocked my world. I couldn't imagine the dojo without him. And yet I knew it was the next vital stepping stone on my journey.

Sensei left the dojo in the care of Les-san and me. In a few hours, I packed my gi bag and went to the dojo. Our Friday night class started at 6:30, and I would be teaching.

**Your Turn**: You may want to take a bit of time to answer the following questions. They may help you capture and explore your own thoughts as they relate to the concepts from this chapter of the journey.

Have you had a time when you felt your soul dying? Are you in that place now?

What can you do to change it?

Can you take steps to make a change that will nurture you instead of drain you?


If you've had a decision made for you that you would not have chosen, can you frame it as a gift or discover the lesson it might hold?

# 教うるは
# 学ぶの半ば

*(Oshiuru wa manabu no nakaba.)*

# Half of teaching is learning (for ourselves).

# 24 The Teacher Is the Student

The next year unfolded as Les-san and I shared teaching responsibilities. I soon learned how much more deeply I needed to understand something to be able to teach it.

Rather than see this as daunting, I welcomed it. Instead of teaching my favorite techniques, the ones that seemed to flow naturally from my body, like Yokomen Uchi Shiho Nage and Morote Dori Tenbin Nage, I started digging into techniques from Shomen Uchi.

This attack straight to the head had often rooted me in place. I found little flow in the straight strong raising of the hand. It seemed so linear, and I often reverted to the same entries and techniques. Off line into Kotegaeshi or Irimi Nage.

In my solo shadow practice, I played with Ato no Sen (moving after the strike) and Sen no Sen (moving before the strike). I explored doing the technique *After* or *With* or *During* the energy of the attack. I envisioned the attack coming in and explored entering inside, or to the side, or to the rear for Sumi Otoshi (Corner Drop).

In time, it became more clear. I could now bring Shomen Uchi to the dojo and start sharing this as a teacher with confidence.

I also continued my solo weapons practice at home, refining my movements and deepening my understanding to bring that to teaching our Kiryu weapons program at the dojo.

Les-san and I took turns teaching and taking each other's classes, learning from each other's approach and strengths. Les-san's career in law enforcement continued to shape my understanding of presence and guiding confidently, not by overpowering the situation but by offering a calm, consistent energy.

**Your Turn**: You may want to take a bit of time to answer the following questions. They may help you capture and explore your own thoughts as they relate to the concepts from this chapter of the journey.

Who are the teachers you learn from the most? Why are they so effective? Are there certain approaches or ways they taught that you can emulate in your teaching?

Are you a teacher, trainer, or coach (regardless of whether this is your title or job description)? What do you enjoy most about it?

If you're interested in teaching, what is the topic you'd like to teach?

When you think about the topic you teach currently or want to teach, what are some aspects of it that you may need to understand better so you can share it? It can be a concept you want to share with family or an idea you'd like to discuss at work as well as in a traditional teacher/student setting.

# 世間は
# 広い様で狭い

*(Seken wa hiroi you de
semai.)*

# The world seems large
# but it's small.

# 25 Setting Sail

The year of 2014 unfurled like a flag waving in the breeze. Class after class, the dojo year continued as Les-san and I taught and as we all Practiced in the dojo. We helped our students along their paths. In the fall, we helped them get ready for their tests.

Along the way, Les-san continued to help with my ukemi. After almost every class, he'd throw me in many breakfalls. Irimi Nage, Ago Ate, Kotegaeshi. Fall after fall, I improved. There was no throw I feared, just some I was better at than others.

Sensei and I talked a couple times a month, usually when I was in my truck in the parking lot waiting to go into the dojo on Friday nights. He'd ask how classes were going. Teaching. Students. If I had questions.

About once a month, I'd ask him if he was ready to open a dojo in California. Every month, he said no.

But in November, a year after he'd moved, during our call he said yes. He was settled in his job, he was buying a house, his family had had a year to adapt to life in a new state. Yes, it was time to open a dojo. Would I like to come help with that?

I answered a solid and definite "Hai." Right then, on Friday night in the parking lot of the dojo, I knew I would be moving.

It was time for me to do something new. After a year of being laid off from my proposal manager position, I was doing freelance but feeling restless. I'd lived in Colorado my whole life, and I was ready for a change.

My parents had retired to the small Kansas town where Mom had grown up, so it wasn't like I'd be leaving them. Now, instead of a day's drive away, I was an airplane flight away. Both would take about the same amount of time, and I would still visit often.

In the next week, I explored options for moving myself, my horses, and some furniture to California, and how to rent out my house in Sedalia.

On a long hike that weekend, I sat on the overlook I often went to. Driving west out of Sedalia to the top of Rampart Range Road, I parked my truck and hiked in a few miles. Sitting on the rock looking over Pike National Forest below, I thought about moving.

Is it really what I wanted to do? Was I running from something or opening to something?

I could see both. Running from boredom and sameness. Opening to new experience, new people, and seeing what might unfold.

I figured that no decision is irrevocable. It was time for me to expand my world and explore what I was capable of.

I started sharing the news with my brothers, Les-san, my neighbors, and friends. Some were shocked – after all, I'd lived in Colorado my whole life. Others understood, and while they'd miss me, they knew it was a step I needed to take.

I waited to share the news in person with my parents during my visit for Thanksgiving.

They understood very well how this was a good move for me. After all, Mom had moved from Kansas to Colorado right after she graduated from college, and Dad had moved a few times while in the  military. And they'd both moved back to Kansas after 60 years in Colorado.

Visiting would mean a plane ride instead of a drive across the midwestern plains.

Yes, daughter, we understand.

I woke up in my new rental near the beach on New Year's Day 2015.

**Your Turn**: You may want to take a bit of time to answer the following questions. They may help you capture and explore your own thoughts as they relate to the concepts from this chapter of the journey.

Is there a big change that's calling to you?

What do you need to do to take it?

# 一寸の光陰軽んず
# べからず

*(Issun no kouin karonzu
bekarazu.)*

Don't belittle a little bit of
time. Every moment is
precious.

# 26 Facing the Unimaginable

Once settled in California, I started looking for dojo space. It wasn't as easy as in Colorado, where Sensei made a few phone calls and had found a new place in a couple weeks.

So we started to Practice in O-Sensei's dojo – on the beach Sunday mornings – and we attended some classes at another Aikido dojo.

Through 2015, training continued. The months blended my Practice, exploring my new state, and working long hours doing technical QA remotely for an e-learning course developer.

On October 14, I was up early working a big project. My cell phone lit up; it was my brother Karl calling from Colorado.

I could tell by his voice something was very, very wrong.

"Kris is gone," he choked out the words. Our brother Kris had taken his life.

We cried with each other on the phone, asking the unanswerable question, "why?" between the silence of sharing this loss too enormous for words.

Kris hadn't left a note. He didn't show up at the family business that morning. He'd been a little stressed about money lately, but no one knew the depth of the pain Kris was in.

After Karl and I said goodbye, I just sat. My legs no longer worked. I just sat, and then the tears came.

Putting sense to this made no sense. My middle brother Kris, so kind, so gentle, so funny. How could he be gone?

I booked a flight to arrive in Colorado the next morning. Sensei's family took me out for dinner that night. I was in another place, floating above the table as the servers brought our meals and filled our water glasses. Everything seemed to have slowed down, way down.

After Kris's service, our family drove to spend time with Mom and Dad in Kansas. Special time, cherished time, as we shared stories and tears and held each other close.

When I got back to California, my dojo family supported me. Calls, walks, checking in. And training. Once again, Aikido was throwing me a lifeline, and I was reaching for it.

**Your Turn**: You may want to take a bit of time to answer the following questions. They may help you capture and explore your own thoughts as they relate to the concepts from this chapter of the journey.

Has an event completely turned your life upside down with grief or pain?

Is there a Practice, a ritual, that you can turn to that will buoy you through this time?

Who can you talk to that can help walk with you in these hard, dark days?

# 旅は道連れ
# 世は情け
*(Tabi wa michizure, you wa nasake.)*

## In traveling, companionship; in life, kindness.

# 27 Bend Like Bamboo

For several years, Dad had been losing more control of his right leg. He'd compensate by walking more slowly, and he had a little stool to help him climb into the cockpit of his Cessna 182. The stool had a cord tied to it, so once Dad was seated at the controls, he pulled up the stool and stowed it in the back seat.

It all seemed normal and just a small blip, nothing that couldn't be worked around.

He started using a cane when he and Mom went out, just in case. But he was able to get around well and still take the weekly drives into the rural Kansas countryside that they both loved.

A couple months after we gathered in Kansas to remember Kris, I visited Mom and Dad for Christmas. I always looked forward to spending time with my folks during the holidays. This year, it was even more special. We were still reeling from losing Kris just a few months before, so it was a gift to have time to share memories, laugh, cry, and just be together. We went for drives, out to eat, and had coffee in our robes every morning. All the normal things we'd always done; the simple the joy of being together.

On Christmas Eve, there was a sprinkle of light snow. Dad thought it might be better if he stayed home and suggested that Mom and I go to church without him. We drove to their little Lutheran

church in the neighboring town of Wilson, marveling at the stars in the winter sky on the drive home.

When we got back and stepped into the warm embrace of their cozy house, we heard Dad say, "Glad you're home," his baritone voice carrying from down the hall. And then, "and maybe you could help me a little bit."

We stepped around the corner and there was Dad, lying on the floor near the bathroom door. He was wearing his robe and had a towel around his bare legs.

"I thought it would be nice to take a hot shower while you were gone," he said. "And after I stepped out and got my robe on, my leg just gave out. It's like it wasn't here."

"So I've just been waiting til you got home. It's pretty comfortable here on the carpet, but maybe you could help me stand up."

I got behind him and hooked my arms under his, doing my best to help him up. I couldn't. His right leg wouldn't bear any weight.

Across the street, the Erichsen's were having their annual Christmas Eve open house. I called Brenda, and asked if Chris and the boys could come over.

In minutes, Chris and another strong neighbor were lifting Dad to his feet and helping him to his chair in the living room. We sat and talked a while, and Dad tried stand up. This time, his leg held. He was able to walk and all was well.

That night was the prelude. Dad's leg became less and less reliable. They traveled to the Mayo Clinic for an evaluation, and Dad was diagnosed with spinal stenosis – narrowing of the spinal column creating nerve impingement.   At Dad's age of 88, they didn't recommend surgery. Thankfully, he didn't have pain.

As winter flowed into spring, Dad lost more ability to walk, even with a walker. Mom and Dad together made that hardest decision. Mom wasn't strong enough to care for Dad alone at home. If he fell, she wouldn't be able to help. They decided that Dad would move to assisted living.

In June 2016, Dad moved first to a care facility about 40 miles away from Mom. It was too far away, but the facility in their little town was full. Dad was on the waiting list. Until a room opened up at the Good Samaritan Home in Ellsworth, Mom drove out every day to see him.

The long drive started taking its toll on Mom. I was afraid she'd fall asleep on the drive back in the dark after dinner. Thankfully, in November, a room was available at Good Sam.

Now just a mile separated Mom and Dad. But they'd never been so far apart.

**Your Turn**: You may want to take a bit of time to answer the following questions. They may help you capture and explore your own thoughts as they relate to the concepts from this chapter of the journey.

Are you facing a shift you never expected, especially with people you love?

Have you witnessed strong people in your life start to become less capable? How can you help them and help yourself deal with the present situation?

How does contemplating the future for someone you care about make you feel about your own future?

If you need to make a difficult decision and neither choice seems good, who can you ask for guidance?

# 歩々これ道場

*(Hobo kore dojo.)*

# A dojo is with every step.

# 28 Another Step on the Journey

2017 began like every other year. My weeks unfolded with Aikido, work, visiting Eddie, calling my parents. Repeat. Life was good and I was enjoying the rhythm that had settled in.

Around mid-year, Sensei shared that he was thinking of recommending Les-san and me to test for Sandan, third-degree black belt, in December.

It was up to us. We had a lot of work to do to prepare for the test, but he believed we would be ready.

As I began to prepare for my Sandan test, I Practiced to honor Kris. I brought his kindness and compassion to my Practice, both for myself and others.

I Practiced to honor my Dad. He was my rock, my mentor. He'd taught me how to pursue dreams and keep working toward them. And now that he couldn't walk on his own, I Practiced to honor his bravery facing this major shift in the direction of his life.

I Practiced to honor my Mom. Her grace and strength amid huge and previously unimaginable change were lights leading the way. Her ability to face with courage both her separation from her soul mate and her continuing struggles with worsening COPD inspired me to live life the best I could and see the positives.

And I Practiced to honor myself. I brought new thankfulness to my ability to walk, to move, to breathe, to do normal things. I honored how far I'd come, and how far I had to go. I didn't take any of it for granted any more.

Through the months of Practice ahead, I worked with John-san and Daniel-san in our California dojo. Each brought different strengths to deepen my Practice, whether it was height, body type, variations in ukemi styles, and experience level. I also attended classes at Aikido

Central Coast and worked out with their students and Senseis.

Sensei and I traveled to train with the Colorado dojo in the summer. Les-san and I got to Practice together a lot, polishing for our tests and pushing each other. We would be each other's Ukes for part of our Sandan tests. I also had the opportunity to Practice with other Colorado students who I'd asked to be part of my test.

Since I first started with Kiryu Aikido, I'd seen and experienced first-hand how "it takes a dojo" to prepare a student for testing. We can't Practice alone, and the journey of improvement while preparing for a test takes all students along in the flow. All boats rise when testing is approached in a positive way.

Finally, December arrived and Les-san and I would be testing. Arriving at Izawa Sensei's dojo at the Boulder YMCA that morning, I was ready. And I was looking forward to the opportunity to share this time with other Aikidoists, many of whom I'd known since my first months of Practice.

For the first part of the test, Sensei called out the technique category. My Uke attacked and I responded with the technique, starting with kneeling techniques of Suwari Waza. The test then moved to Hanmi Handachi, where I was kneeling and Uke was standing for the attacks.

Tachi Waza was next – standing techniques. I used several Ukes for this phase, both to not exhaust one person and also for the opportunity to show techniques with Ukes of different sizes, body types, experience levels. There's nothing more joyful than flowing with your partner as a two-person team through strong, martial techniques.

Weapons came next. First bokken, then jo, then tanto. Les-san was my Uke for my weapons section, as I was for his. He came in with strong, committed attacks. I entered in and finished each technique, showing a range of Futokoro (inside) and Tamoto (outside) techniques. We finished with Jo Nage, where I had the weapon and threw Les-san.

"Hai. Seiza," said Sensei. I kneeled in seiza on one end of the mat facing my Ukes on the other. We took a few deep breaths before the final part of my test began: Randori with multiple attackers. Because I was testing for Sandan, I would have more attackers than in my previous tests.

As I took one more deep breath, I was ready to do my best and bring the layers of Randori I'd been practicing over the past few months.

Be aware of where you are on the mat. Don't get trapped in a corner. Move around (own) the mat to your advantage. Know where all your attackers are. Anticipate where they might attack. Don't be caught off guard. If you're getting trapped, slip through a gap.

And perhaps the most challenging layer – vary the techniques and finish the techniques as much as possible.

It's easy, especially after a few minutes when your lungs are burning and brain is on overload, to get sloppy and resort to just deflecting attackers and getting out of the way – essentially just staying alive. But it's much more effective and shows a higher level of training

to respond to the incoming attack with a technique that makes sense. Finish it, then move on and take care of the next attack. While you don't want to do Otoshi Waza – pressure techiques like Ikkyo that end in a pin on the mat – because they take too long and leave you exposed, many other techniques can be used quickly and effectively in Randori. Kotegaeshi, Shiho Nage, Irimi Nage, Kokyo Nage, Tenbin Nage, and more.

"Start whenever you're ready," said Sensei. I quickly bowed to my Ukes lined up at the edge of the mat and called out "Hajime!" Begin!

I was on my feet and moving toward my attackers instead of waiting for them to come to me. "Sakoi!" I said to myself. I invited each attack, entered in, responded. Slipped through an opening, and faced my attackers from a new direction.

Attack, technique, attack, blend, attack, technique, attack, reposition. A blur of movement. Incoming attacks of Shomen Uchi, Yokomen Uchi, Tsuki. Techniques depending on the angle, timing, range, spacing. Time slowed. I could see and sense the attacks and be in the right position. Unlike Randori in past classes and mock tests, I felt like I could go and go. I wasn't spent; I was breathing, relaxed.

"Hai! Yame!" I heard Sensei's voice from somewhere that sounded far away. The sound brought me back to the mat, to the Randori, to my test.

My Ukes lined up again on one side and I faced them.

Ota gai ni rei

Sensei ni rei.

Shomen ni rei.

My Sandan test was complete.

I fell asleep that night tired, sore, and so filled with joy and gratitude. Spending the day doing the martial art I loved with the people I trusted, respected, and valued was truly a gift.

I was glad my test was over and for the opportunity to share my Aikido. I was proud of the test. I'd prepared well and felt I'd brought the best I could to that sliver of time on the mat. I also knew what I wanted to focus on when I returned to Practice and where I wanted to improve.

As soon as I got back to California, it was time to get back on the mat and back to Practice. Not with the focus of my next test, but with the intent to keep learning, keep growing, keep moving, keep flowing with whatever came next.

What I didn't know was that the real tests in my life were soon to follow.

**Your Turn**: You may want to take a bit of time to answer the following questions. They may help you capture and explore your own thoughts as they relate to the concepts from this chapter of the journey.

What is a significant milestone or event you have coming up?

How can you augment your Practice? Who can you call on to help you prepare?

As you prepare, can you focus on honoring someone else with your Practice? Who would that be, and why?

# ならぬ堪忍
# するが堪忍

*(Naranu kannin suru ga kannin.)*

## To patiently endure what is unendurable is true endurance.

# 29 Facing the Future

For two years, Mom visited Dad every day at the nursing home. Often she'd sneak in a mason jar of wine and they'd share it while watching a movie in Dad's room. She brought the local weekly newspaper and the mail, which they'd open together so Dad was part of the small details of their life.

She decorated his room for each holiday. On sunny days when Dad was feeling up to it, she'd maneuver his wheelchair out to the garden area where they could sit and feel the sun on their shoulders and watch the birds and flowers.

The only thing that kept them apart was an occasional Kansas ice storm, or when Mom was in the hospital with pneumonia. Each episode further damaged her lungs, already compromised by her worsening COPD.

By June 2018, Dad was fading fast. His light was dimming. The saddest, hardest thing was that Mom wasn't able to be with him. She was in the hospital with another bout of pneumonia.

On their 65th wedding anniversary, June 14, their aides were angels, connecting Mom and Dad with Facetime so they could see each other. Dad couldn't talk, but he smiled.

On Father's Day, June 17, 2018, Dad died.

Losing Dad hit me so, so hard. I was grateful he was no longer imprisoned by a body that did not work, but I missed him so much. My teacher, my friend, my mentor. Gone.

We had two services for Dad. One in Ellsworth, Kansas. One in Evergreen, Colorado. At both, I shared an essay I wrote to describe Dad and what he brought to the world. One of the biggest things was his belief in pursuing your passion, whatever it was. Not taking the "safe" route that society or your culture dictated as the best course of action if it did not also feed your soul. "Follow your dreams," he always said. "The money will follow."

He and Mom had shown that in creating the family business that still thrives today with my brothers Kurt and Karl now owning the business.

He also believed in helping others pursue their dreams, and he and Mom helped in many anonymous ways to help others to do just that.

Mom adjusted to life without Dad and their daily visits. Maybe it was her midwestern roots that made her so strong, like those of the plains willows, bending in the storms but never toppling.

Losing her best friend was deeply hard on her, and yet she carried on with such grace and softness and strength. When I'd come visit several times a year, we'd talk and reminisce about their adventures and life together. And we talked about Mom's life and her passions. She continued to play her Appalachian Dulcimer with the local bluegrass group. She played bells in her church. She quilted up a storm, making each of us kids a custom quilt and creating small seasonal quilts she designed.

Those days of visiting Mom were gifts. Quiet, unassuming gifts.

One of my greatest joys was driving Mom around town for errands and outings in her 1998 Mercedes Benz. She loved having a driver, and said often how wonderful it was to be spoiled.

One cold November when I was visiting for Thanksgiving, we drove to the bank so she could make a deposit and get some cash. The drive-through had the pneumatic tubes and the teller behind the window talking into the speaker. As we sat waiting for the canister to whoosh back into the holder, Mom shared something. I'd never heard her say it, but I'd seen her live it every day of her life. I'm not sure what triggered the conversation, but I will remember it always.

"You know, it's not very hard to be kind," she said, "yet so many people struggle with it."

A whoosh of air announced the tube was sending the canister on its way back. I swiveled opened the plastic door and handed the cash and deposit slip to Mom. She held it in her hands, covered in red leather gloves, on her lap.

"I've always believed my job every day is to see how I can help lighten someone's day," she said. "It doesn't have to be a big thing. Even a little thing – like a smile – can make a big difference."

Our next stop was Gene's Heartland Foods, the local IGA grocery store, to shop for our Thanksgiving meal.

One of the best things about a small town is that everyone knows each other. Maybe it's the slower pace that helps people seem to be more willing to take the time to help.

We loaded up on shrimp, a beautiful turkey, yams, fresh green beans, fresh beets, canned pumpkin, and half-and-half for our morning coffee. A bag of cinnamon candy to make Mom's spiced apples, and a head of red cabbage to make our family recipe of Danish warm red cabbage. I remembered how much Dad especially loved these two dishes during the holidays.

The young man who bagged our groceries put each full bag back in the cart. After Mom paid, he swiveled the cart out of the way and waited. As Mom and I slowly walked to the car, he pushed it along behind us, remarking how cold it was for November, but thankfully there wasn't much snow in the forecast.

Mom's left hand was tucked safely in the crook of my elbow. Her right hand held the portable oxygen concentrator that went with her whenever she was away from home. We made our way across the light snow dusting the parking lot.

He opened the door to Mom's car and carefully put the grocery bags on the back seat. He shut the door and wheeled the cart around to take it back to the store. "Have a wonderful Thanksgiving, Mrs. Andersen, and stay warm," he said.

"Thank you," she said. "You're always so helpful to me and I appreciate you always carrying out my groceries." Mom pulled out the $50 bill she'd gotten from the bank and handed it to him. "Here's a little something. I hope you have a happy Thanksgiving."

"Gosh, Mrs. Andersen, thank you!" he grinned. "I love helping you. You're always so nice. Happy Thanksgiving to you and your daughter!"

I went out to the barn to visit Eddie a few times a week. I chose evenings – when the barn was quiet and the sound of horses chewing their hay blended with twilight birdsong – and on the weekends, usually after Aikido on Sunday mornings. The time we spent followed a lovely rhythm.

As I'd round the shady corner on the way to his pen and came into view, Eddie would lift his head, prick up his ears, and whinny. I never, ever got tired of his greeting, and no matter what was on my mind, his hello made me smile, and I called "Hello, Eddie!" back to my kind, brown horse.

Eddie would dip his nose into the green halter I held, waiting while I buckled the strap around his strong, mahogany neck. Then I'd push open his gate and we'd go for a walk on the trails around the barn.

Often after our walks, or sometimes instead if I was filling his feed ration bags for the next week, I'd turn him into the outdoor arena.

If he was feeling frisky that day, he might trot or canter around a bit. But it never took long for him to head to the soft ground in the middle of the arena. He loved to roll. He'd roll on one side, stand up, and roll on the other.

Then he'd shake – that whole-horse shake that started at the tip of his ears and went to very tip of his tail. Then he'd often lie down again for a nap. Even more than rolling, Eddie loved lying down in the sun and napping.

He could lie down in his pen, and often did, but the arena was wide open napping freedom.

In the early years, Eddie's napping was frequent and uneventful. But as Eddie rounded the corner past his late 20s and headed toward his 30th birthday, getting up from his joyful naps became harder and harder.

It was painful to watch him struggle to get to his feet. Sometimes it took several tries for him to stand up, but other times, as if to say "Hey, don't worry about me!" he'd pop right up.

Eventually, though, it was always a struggle getting up. I swear I could see him thinking, "Should I lie down? I really, really, really want to, but it's so hard to get up."

He started getting cast in his pen overnight – unable to stand up on his own. For a horse, being down is deeply stressful. They're prey animals, and when their ability to stand and run fast and far away from danger is gone, first they panic. Then they give up. Watching this look on Eddie's face – of deep fear and then resignation to dying – was the hardest thing to witness. Plus, a horse that lies down too long can cut off circulation to their legs and cause muscle damage and eventual kidney failure.

A few mornings, Roberto at the barn would find Eddie down. He'd usually be able to get him up by putting on his halter and pulling hard, but it wasn't easy.

There was also no telling how long Eddie had been down, in the cold, in the dark, alone. My biggest fear was that he would die this way. Afraid. Alone.

It was time for me to make that hardest, most painful decision – to let Eddie go and free him from the possibility of a horrible end that he did not deserve.

On August 26, 2019, a bright, sunny morning, I arrived at the barn. Eddie and I went for a walk up our favorite trail. When we got back, I had a bowl of soaked senior feed waiting for him. Normally he got just a bit of the sweeter senior feed to make the rest of his soaked hay pellets and beet pulp more palatable. Today, he got a big sloppy yummy pan of soaked senior feed.

My friend Kacey arrived a little later. Eddie's pen was between Kacey's horses Chief and Star. They were all great friends, and we often turned them out together. Kacey offered to be with us as Eddie and I said goodbye that day, and I gratefully hugged her in thanks.

Eddie slurped his feed as we waited for Dr. Osborne. He'd been Eddie's vet for most of the time Eddie had been in California, and he was a key player on Eddie's wellness team. And now he was here to do that final, kindest, most difficult job for a vet who loves his patients as he does his own horses.

As I held his lead rope, Eddie's soft breath on my neck whispered that our connection wouldn't end when he was no longer here.

He went peacefully and I was grateful he was again running free in knee-high grass, rolling, and taking long, sweet naps in the sun.

Eddie and I had been together 22 years, and his passing devastated me. He'd been with me in all the phases of my life – early marriage, meeting Mark Rashid and becoming his students, growing together in our connection and partnership. He listened to my confusion and pain as my marriage upended and unraveled. He accepted with kindness and softness when I moved him and Serena three times in two years after I left my marriage, as well as the big cross-country move with strangers on a commercial shipper to join me in California.

Eddie was always there. His strong, wise presence; his lack of worry at whatever life presented; his joy in the simple, real things – riding often before his hoof injury, going for walks together, eating his soaked food, chewing on hay and grass, rolling in soft earth, napping in the sun.

With Eddie's passing, I now had lost three strong males in my life within five years. The grief was mounting, and each loss added to the pain I carried with me. All I could do was cherish the time we'd had, hold close the memories, and be thankful that Kris, Dad, and Eddie were all free from the physical and emotional pain that had shackled them on earth.

But after so many losses in just a few years, I was spent.

Once again, the rhythm of Aikido Practice kept me going. Sunday mornings on the beach, Wednesday evening at our dojo space, occasional Practice with other local dojos, traveling to seminars.

Practice gave me a place to go, a place beyond the darkness that was becoming a frequent companion. Practice grounded me in its sameness yet newness. Every class had the same structure, but every class was new.

I could find comfort in the familiar but not go on autopilot.

As summer turned to fall, I started feeling a bit better, but a new dread was beginning.

In my daily phone calls with Mom, I could tell things were changing. She was having more not-so-good breathing days, which she attributed to the late summer heat and humidity.

But she was still ever gracious and uncomplaining. She'd share stories of the twins, Logan and Noah, next door coming to visit, and their parents Brenda and Chris checking in often. Spending time with her best friend Dorothy when they could. Doing errands, enjoying neighbors who'd stop by for a visit. Life in Ellsworth rolled along on its comforting, slower pace.

We started to make plans for my Christmas trip. In one of those conversations, I wondered out loud about gathering our family together this year. We all hadn't been together for Christmas since before they moved to Ellsworth in 2011, and the last time our family had gathered was for their 60th anniversary in 2013.

Mom loved the idea, and I set out to talk to my brothers and sisters-in-law so they could start planning. I shared how excited Mom was by the idea, and asked if everyone would consider coming out. The response was heartening – nearly everyone would be there.

For several days before and after Christmas, 11 people and three dogs filled Mom and Dad's little house with so much love.

Mom was absolutely luminous surrounded by her family. Spending time doing nothing but basking in the deep goodness of being together filled her with light.

On New Year's Day 2020, I called to wish Mom a happy new year. She sounded tired but was looking forward to the year. We talked

about my visit in April for her 92nd birthday, and how much we looked forward to it.

A few weeks later, Mom was in the hospital. Again. Another bout of pneumonia. More lung damage, more progression of her COPD.

After she got home, we talked about me coming to visit – soon, in addition to the visit in April. News on the other side of the world was starting to spread the images from China with full hospitals and stymied doctors who didn't know what was causing this deadly sickness… the thing they were calling COVID-19.

"No, honey," she said. "I think it's too dangerous for you to travel. I don't want you to risk getting sick."

Then she added, "I'm doing fine, and Dr. Slomka is taking really good care of me."

Things happened fast after that. Another trip to the hospital, and setting up home healthcare visits. A call from Dr. Slomka telling me in his heavy accent what was going on with my dear Mom in medical terms that did nothing but confuse me. And even if I'd understood, I didn't want to hear it.

Losing Mom was something I'd been dreading for years. I could not imagine living without my Mom, our daily calls, frequent visits.

Our connection. The absolute knowing of her love for me, and my love for her.

Losing her was more than I could bear.

At the same time, COVID was racing around the world, destroying families and communities in its wake.

The uncertainty of all this – a world in crisis and my Mom's compounding and likely terminal health struggles – was coming to a head.

In California, the stay-at-home order began March 17. Mom went to the hospital on March 22 in one more attempt to remove fluid from her lungs and to help the edema release from her body. She was fine, she said. When I and other family called and said that we'd be out in a day to see her, she was adamant.

She didn't want any of us to risk traveling to see her. She didn't want us to get sick. She was doing all right, she said, and Dr. Slomka and everyone at the hospital was taking great care of her.

Because the hospital wasn't allowing in visitors who weren't immediate family, Logan and Noah and their best friend Adam brought their trumpet, trombone, and euphonium to play outside of her hospital room window. The nurses wheeled Mom to the window so she could see her dear young friends and hear their impromptu concert.

She waved and smiled, and held her hands on her heart as she listened.

These two boys had adopted Mom and Dad when they moved in across the street 10 years before. They'd been like her own kids, stopping in for visits, taking out the trash, shoveling the driveway, mowing the lawn, bringing over their dates for prom and homecoming so she could see them all dressed up.

The staff and several patients of the little hospital gathered at the windows as they played, and some came outside to watch and listen.

No one held back the tears as they walked back inside the little community hospital on the Kansas prairie.

The next few days were a downward spiral as the complications from heart disease and COPD converged. The hospital finally agreed to let Brenda come visit and sit with Mom.

On March 27, 2020, with Brenda at her side, Mom raised her arms one last time and smiled. I think Dad and Kris were coming to bring her home.

**Your Turn**: You may want to take a bit of time to answer the following questions. They may help you capture and explore your own thoughts as they relate to the concepts from this chapter of the journey.

When life throws you into a spiral of loss, how do you keep from drowning?

Does your life keep bringing grief after grief?

When you've endured so much change and so much pain, how do you cope? How do you carry on?

Can your Practice help you stay grounded? It won't, and it can't, take away the pain of loss, but it may help give you a quiet place to rest.

# 昔は昔, 今は今

*(Mukashi wa mukashi, ima wa ima.)*

# The past is the past, and now is now.

# 30 The World Shifts

At the same time that I was reeling from losing my Mom, so sad and so angry that I hadn't been with her when she died, I – like everyone else – was reeling from COVID. The uncertainty, the confusion, the fear we collectively felt in March 2020 brought us all to our knees.

Where were we going? What was going to happen? When would this end? Would this end?

With stay-at-home orders in place, we closed the dojo.

Not having Aikido as the steady place in my life was agony. I worked on my weapons techniques and we all kept in touch with texts.

In those months without Practice, I felt adrift. Aikido had been the one thing in my life I could count on to always be there. A steady place to ground and stop the swirling from life.

Without it, I didn't know which end was up.

When summer came, we started meeting in a park. At least we could do our weapons techniques with distance between us.

Getting back to Practice, even just an hour a week, started bringing normalcy back to life.

---

**Your Turn**: You may want to take a bit of time to answer the following questions. They may help you capture and explore your own thoughts as they relate to the concepts from this chapter of the journey.

How did you cope with the pandemic, as life changed and everything we'd known as normal was gone?

Did you have a Practice that helped you get through?

# 健全なる精神は健全なる身体に宿る

*(Kenzen naru seishin wa kenzen naru shintai ni yadoru.)*

# A healthy mind resides in a healthy body.

# 31 Leaning into Practice, Part II

Taking the unwanted break from Practice during much of 2020 and 2021 shifted many things. Going from five or six hours of intense training a week to zero, and the unrelenting stress of losing half my family, my horse, and dealing with the deep unknowns of COVID started affecting my health.

My body reacted in unsurprising but disturbing ways: sky-high cortisol levels, rising cholesterol, unrelenting fatigue, depression, weight gain, and muscle loss. I'd always had a trim and tiny waist. I thought it was something I'd always have without needing to work at it. But age, COVID, stress, and lack of activity proved otherwise.

I also started feeling more forgetful. I had to write everything down, and even then, I'd forget to do things. It was a scary time.

Eventually COVID retreated and our dojo began to Practice again. We resumed our Sunday morning Practice on the beach and continued our weeknight weapons Practice at the park. Eventually, we sublet space at another dojo to Practice on Friday nights. It felt so good to have the cool mats under my feet, and the opportunity to take rolls and polish off the square edges of my body that had returned with lack of Practice on tatami mats.

I started noticing more aches and pains than I remembered from Practice, but ironically, more Practice meant fewer aches and pains.

After enduring so many losses and life changes over the past six years, returning to my Practice helped me start recovering my health and finding me again. It gave me a solid surface on which to stand.

It also reaffirmed how much I love this martial art and how much I want my Practice of Aikido to be in my life until I'm 80 or 90 years old, God willing.

**Your Turn**: You may want to take a bit of time to answer the following questions. They may help you capture and explore your own thoughts as they relate to the concepts from this chapter of the journey.

Has your health been affected by the pandemic or other major life changes? What have you experienced?

How can you make small changes to regain the health you desire?

What did you learn during the pandemic that can keep you healthy into the future?

Do you have a vision of how you want to age and the qualities you want to keep now for the years ahead?

# 柳に雪折れなし

*(Yanagi ni yukiore nashi.)*

Willow trees don't break
under the weight of snow.

# 32 Beginner's Mind, Part II

Our dojo had tested with Kei and Mariquita Izawa Senseis for almost as long as I'd been training with Kiryu Aikido. After the pandemic, though, Izawa Sensei was feeling the desire to pull back from testing other dojos.

He suggested one option was to join Hendricks Sensei's Division 1 of the California Aikido Association. Based on the long and positive history between Sensei and Hendricks Sensei, it made sense.

Many years before, Sensei had met Hendricks Sensei when she was invited to teach at Nippon Kan dojo in Denver, where he was Chief Instructor.

More recently, we'd been to several of her biannual seminars in San Leandro, and I'd been Uchi Deshi again for a week after I moved to California.

Over the next few months, Kiryu Aikido transitioned to become a dojo with Hendricks Sensei's group and we started training in earnest with them.

In addition to regular testing of kyu and dan ranks, Hendricks Sensei offered the opportunity to test under her Iwama weapons curriculum. Because of her dedication and decades of learning from Morihiro Saito Sensei, she had been awarded the Menkyo Kaiden – the highest level of weapons technique transmission. To this day, she carries forward Saito Sensei's lineage and teachings through her dojo and separate weapons program.

Sensei and I dove in to learning this weapons style. We already had a strong weapons program in Kiryu Aikido which was Iwama based. With four basic relations, both bokken to bokken and bokken to jo, six intermediate relations, and four detailed paired kata with bokken and jo, our program was robust.

Adding Hendricks Sensei's weapons program would be a logical next step for the dojo and the continued growth of Kiryu students as Aikidoists.

With the purchase of Hendricks Sensei's Black Belt Essentials online course created with Aikido Journal, Sensei and I started practicing the first five techniques of Kumi Jo (jo to jo), Kumi Tachi (bokken to bokken), and Ken Tai Jo (bokken to jo).

While a lot of the individual moves were similar, the combinations and footwork were quite different.

With the first Practice of this new weapons style, I was yanked back into old familiar territory. I was a complete beginner again. But this time, with 16 years of muscle memory and a brain in my late 50s, to say learning new weapons techniques was challenging would be a huge understatement.

The demons I'd faced on the mat at different times over the years came racing back, and they were screaming. I'm no good at this. I'll never get this. I'm disappointing Sensei. I'm holding him back because I don't learn as quickly as he does.

Then, if I felt what I perceived as frustration rising because I wasn't getting a technique – even though we'd just done it five times, or 10 or 25 times – the demons screamed louder and made it even harder to concentrate.

Not only were the demons screaming but they often brought tears with them. After more than a few Practices, I'd drive home, tears streaming down my face. Tears of deep shame and never being good enough or smart enough. I was angry and frustrated and demoralized at myself. Feeling stupid, inept, and incapable. The self-loathing went deep. I knew that tears were not part of being a martial artist, but there they were.

And then the internal dialogue began.

What's the point? I'll never get this. Why am I putting myself through agony? This is not enjoyable, and it just keeps showing me again and again my inadequacies and slowness in learning new things. Why not just quit?

Aikido is hard for me. My brain doesn't see patterns easily, and replicating what I see with my eyes into my body as movement has always been difficult. And now, getting older, it was like I'd see a move, do it, and then completely forget what I'd just done a few seconds before. Retaining the memory was fleeting, and where a movement had been now was just a blank, black hole of nothingness.

Part of me was ready to quit. It wasn't worth the pain and the continual reminder of my inadequacy as a martial artist. I'd never measure up, and I'd rather concentrate on refining and deepening the Kiryu weapons program that I'd been practicing for 16 years. It was part of me; it was held in my muscle memory.

Another part of me was ready to say, "I will not give up, and I'll learn this system even if it kills me."

Dramatic? Very.

The problem was that I never knew from one session to the next which part of me would show up. I did know this: my emotions and the darkness this had triggered ran deep. The voices weren't going to be brushed aside or told to be quiet. Those techniques had worked for me in the past, but they wouldn't work now. In fact, I could tell that the old approach likely would backfire.

I had to face the demons once again. But this time, it wasn't to conquer them. It was to hear what they wanted to tell me. What was the lesson? What was the learning?

**Your Turn**: You may want to take a bit of time to answer the following questions. They may help you capture and explore your own thoughts as they relate to the concepts from this chapter of the journey.

Have you been tempted to give up because the pain of facing inadequacy was just too painful? What was the situation?

When you're learning something new, especially as you get older, do you have demons shouting at you? Are they the same demons from earlier in life, or are they new? What are they saying?

Are the messages that you are hearing true for now, or are they old scripts and stories?

# 精神一到何事か成らざらん

*(Seishin itto nanigoto ka narazaran.)*

# Nothing is impossible to a willing heart.

# 33 Listening to Wisdom from Unlikely Places

When the tears stopped and I could get quiet, I started to hear the messages behind them.

To be gentle with myself. To know that I learn as fast as I learn, and that my learning can't be rushed. To know that I can do this; it just may take me longer. And like in all my previous years of Practice, I'll just have to work harder, be more stubborn, be more consistent, than anyone else. That's the way it is. And I need to accept it.

I also realized that to start doing the best I could, I needed to bring within myself the same energy I'd felt in Mark Rashid when he's working with horses. I needed to figure out how to keep my stress level low, to back off my internalized pressure when things got intense, to build in "soak" time to learn a movement.

I knew that when I got overwhelmed or over-stressed, my brain would shut down. Trauma, whether real or imagined, would short-circuit my ability to learn. When my empathic antennae picked up a shift in energy from positive to frustrated during a weapons session, I'd go into retreat mode and shut down to keep myself safe. I learned this during my marriage. For good or for bad, it was now wired into me.

So I started by backing off my self-imposed pressure. It wasn't easy. I focused on the movement and the moment, and kept coming back to that. If my mind started down the path of "I'll never be good at this," with the rising feelings of overwhelm, shame, and frustration, I'd gently say to myself, "Stay here. You're safe. You're doing fine."

Every session wasn't perfect. I still ping-ponged between "I can do this!" and "I will never learn this." But I could see the positive difference this new approach was making. The frustrating sessions became fewer, and I started adding layers to the initial understanding.

Some sessions, I was able to do all five Kumi Jo or all five Kumi

Tachi, both as Uke and Nage. I knew the movements that came next.

No longer was there always a black hole of nothingness when I couldn't remember what we had just done. It popped up now and then, but much less frequently.

There were sessions when we'd walk to our cars afterwards and I was filled with the positive feelings of progress and understanding. And the tears when I was driving home? Those no longer came with me after class.

One huge way I knew I was learning came when we attended a seminar with Hendricks Sensei in Colorado late in 2022. There were many students attending who had never done her weapons style, and some who had barely picked up a bokken before.

Suddenly, I was the Sempai. I understood the basic five techniques and was able to share that knowledge. I was helping other students learn the techniques: how to strike, which direction to go, what happens next. I couldn't believe it and it felt great.

Of course, when Hendricks Sensei moved beyond the first five techniques, I felt a bit lost again. But this time, I picked one of my Sempai to work with so I could continue learning, and I didn't feel like I was holding them back. I felt like we were all learning and practicing

Now I'm able to step back and look at the past several months. I've come so far, and I am proud of that. I have made progress. I own the work I've put in. I'm thankful for Sensei's teaching and the opportunity to work alongside him as we both continue to learn and get further on this path together.

I have hope now. Over time, I'm confident that I will learn all the techniques. I'll learn them deeply, just like I've learned the Kiryu weapons techniques.

And now, I also know that I will learn… at the pace I learn. I will honor the way I learn, the way my brain works, and the time I need for movements to become part of my muscle memory.

I can't rush the process. That will only awaken the demons, who are dozing peacefully now. All I can do is make the choice to take another step, and another, and another, be gentle with myself, and continue on the path.

That is the Way of being a martial artist. Keep going, keep growing, keep reaching for the goals you have and the person you want to become.

I'm proud of sticking with it and how much I've learned in just a few months. Mostly I'm proud of facing my demons and listening to their wisdom. I know they have my best interests at heart.

**Your Turn**: You may want to take a bit of time to answer the following questions. They may help you capture and explore your own thoughts as they relate to the concepts from this chapter of the journey.

If you're learning something new and your demons are shouting, what might be the messages they are telling you?

What are some ways you can set yourself up for success, based on your unique way of learning?

# 七転び八起き

*(Nana korobi, ya oki.)*

# Fall down seven times, stand up eight.

# 34 Bowing in to Life

As you can see, I've been a most unlikely student of Aikido. For whatever reason, I've stuck with it.

Through the challenges and uncomfortableness – and joyful growth – and doing my best to accept with grace the physical shifts that come with spending more years on the earth, I have changed. My life has changed. The way I deal with challenge has changed.

I'm more able to flow with What Is, not worry so much about What If, and face what's ahead of me. Like in Randori, there's no use trying to ward off attacks that haven't happened yet. All I can do is be ready for what comes in and work with it in the moment.

Through all these years, my Practice has buoyed me in rough waters. Aikido is the lifeline that pulls me through. It gives me a place to go, to ground, to center. To be around people who will be there. Not to coddle me, but to walk with me. And I with them.

Its challenges have made me stronger, more resilient. Better able to flow and bend and survive the storms of life.

What's next? I don't know. None of us know. The only thing that's for sure is that life is ephemeral. It's fleeting. What we know as normal today may change drastically tomorrow.

I know that I'm deep in the current of life. As I flow through the days in my little canoe, I know I have an oar. I can steer a bit, make certain choices and not make other ones. And mostly, I can accept and flow with the current of the river that provides the power, knowing it will bring me to exactly where I'm supposed to be next.

I also know that my training, my Practice, will help me to face and deal with whatever comes next.

I've learned that if I show up, Practice will continue to hone the qualities I'd like to bring with me in the rest of my journey. Bravery. Courage. Dedication. Gratitude. Perseverance. Service. Humility.

And Love. The deep, ever-present Love that connects life and all of us in community of being human and being alive.

The future will take care of itself. For now, it's time to get back to Practice. The dojo of life is open 24/7. The next class starts now.

I change into my gi. Tie my belt. Pull on my hakama, wrapping the himo around the back and tying them tight in the front.

I bow in.

Onegaishimasu.

I'll see you in the dojo.

**Your Turn**: You may want to take a bit of time to answer the following questions. They may help you capture and explore your own thoughts as they relate to the concepts from this chapter of the journey.

What's next for you?

What do you yearn to bring to the next days or years of your life?

What do you love?

What do you want to do more of?

What do you want to focus energy on, or release energy from?

At the end of your life, what would you most love to have done? What are the steps you can begin to bring this to reality?

# Wherever your path leads, may your journey be filled with strength and wisdom, hope and peace.

# Afterword

Aikido has helped me learn not just techniques, how to fall, and some Japanese language, but how to navigate life a little better.

In the years after I left my marriage, some things – life-threatening things that no one could have seen coming, and no one would have wished on anyone – have happened in John's life. When I heard the news, in those crystalline moments something arose from the ashes of what had been. It was compassion. The pure caring about the well-being of a fellow human being.

It took the strength I'd gained from Aikido to leave my marriage so we both could find a different, and better, way forward. And it took the fragile, tender heart of a warrior to let myself understand how we're all imperfect beings making our way through life. We do the best we can with what we have to work with. It may not be pretty, but it's all we've got in the moment.

Without me leaving, we never would have gotten to this better place of understanding and support of each other. Now I am able to look back, cherish the learning, appreciate the time we shared and the lessons, and understand we all come into people's lives for a reason.

Through my Practice, I have also come to understand deeply what true friendship means, and maybe what the Samurai felt with their chosen companions in battle and life.

Along the road that's led me to Aikido, I've met lifelong friends: my Samurai. These are people I know I can count on. No matter when, no matter what. I trust them with my life. We walk together, strong on our own, and together our strength is multiplied.

We support each other's journeys, each other's challenges, each other's triumphs. I can't imagine life without my Samurai.

And the journey continues.

# 人生意気に感ず

*(Jinsei iki ni kanzu.)*

# Life is felt by the spirit/heart.

# Glossary

## Horse terms

**Bay**: A common horse color with a brown body and black mane, tail, and lower legs.

**Bridle**: Headgear used to guide a horse when riding or driving; the entire headgear assembly including headstall, bit, and reins.

**Canter**: A three-beat gait; it has the same footfalls as the western lope.

**Cue**: A signal from the rider that requests the horse to respond with a certain movement. The signal can be from a natural aid (hands, seat, leg, voice, weight, mind, intention, focus, center, energy) or artificial aid (whip, crop, spur, halter, chain).

**Diagonal**: The movement of a foreleg in unison with the opposite hind leg. At the jog or trot, the left front and right hind legs move together in a diagonal, and vice versa.

**English**: A style of riding and equipment that uses a flat English saddle without the deep seat, high cantle or saddle horn that are part of a Western saddle. The rider uses two hands on the reins, rather than one as is typical with western riding. The three broad styles of English riding are hunt seat, saddle seat, and dressage, and saddles are made specifically for different English styles.

**Flying lead change**: In the lope or canter, the horse changes leads in midair with no steps of walk or jog in the transition.

**Green horse or green rider**: A horse or rider who is either young or inexperienced; not fully trained.

**Gymkhana games**: Informal speed games, contests, and races on horseback.

**Halter**: Refers both to the headgear worn by a horse that allows the horse to be led with a lead rope, as well as the horse show class, where the horse is judged on conformation, type, and quality of breed standards.

**Hand**: Traditional form of measuring a horse. A hand is about 4 inches, and is measured from the ground to the top of the horse's withers.

**Jog**: The term used in western riding for a two-beat diagonal gait that has the same footfall as the trot. The right front and left hind move as a pair, and the left front and right hind move together as a pair.

**Lateral work**: Sideways movement, varying from completely sideways in the sidepass to maintaining sideways movement while going forward in the leg yield.

**Lead**: The foreleg that takes the longer stride while the horse is at the lope or canter indicates which "lead" he is on. A horse is on the left lead if the left leg reaches farther in the lope or canter, and on the right lead when the right leg reaches further in the lope or canter. When the horse is traveling clockwise, he will be on the right lead, and vice versa.

**Leg yield**: The horse moves forward and sideways at the same time, crossing the forelegs and hind legs to the front.

**Longe (or lunge)**: Working a horse on a long line, usually with a long whip used as an extension of the hand, and with the handler standing in the middle of the pen.

**Lope**: A three-beat gait with the same in footfall as the canter. If the horse is on the left lead, the footfall is right hind, the left hind and right front landing together, then left front. See also lead.

**Post**: To rise and sit in time with the rhythm of the horse's trot.

**Seat**: The "seat" is a generalized term that refers to the way the rider positions their body while on the horse and allows them to ride in balance and connection with the horse's movement, while also maintaining independent and effective control of legs, aids, and reins.

**Showmanship**: An in-hand (not riding) horse show class where the handler leads and positions the horse with a halter and lead rope. The handler is judged on their skill, awareness, and ability to present their horse to the judge. Compare to halter class.

**Softness**: Allows a horse to respond quietly and quickly to cues and from a position of understanding and willingness rather than compliance and worry.

**Tack**: All the gear used to ride or handle a horse, including halter, lead rope, saddle, pad, bridle, and other equipment.

**Trail class**: a horse show class that involves riding over or negotiating a variety of obstacles that might be found on a trail ride, such as opening a gate from the horse's back, walking over logs, turning around in a small space, carrying a bag of cans, putting on a rain coat, and so on.

**Transition**: A change from one gait to another; for example, from walk to jog, or from jog to lope, or a change within a gait, from a collected jog to an extended jog.

**Trot**: The term used in English riding for a two-beat diagonal gait that has the same footfall as the jog. The right front and left hind move as a pair, and the left front and right hind move together as a pair.

**Walk**: A four-beat gait in which the horse's feet move together on the same side: right hind, right front, then left hind, left front.

**Western**: This style of riding developed from the needs of ranching and livestock management. The saddle is made to distribute weight more evenly over the horse's back for long hours of ranch work as well as counterbalance the pull and weight from a roped cow. Western saddles have a saddle horn to carry a rope, a deep seat for comfort and stability when riding in rough terrain. Today, a variety of western saddles are made specifically for different events such as barrel racing, cutting, reining, roping, and equitation. Compare to English style.

**Withers**: The highest point of the horse's back where the neck and back join.

# Aikido terms

**Ai**: Harmony. First character of Aikido.

**Ai-hanmi**: Both partners having same foot (right or left) forward.

**Aikido**: Ai means harmony or coming together. Ki is spirit or energy. Do means a way or path.

**Aikidoka**: Practitioners of Aikido.

**Atemi**: Punches and other sorts of strikes to your partner's unguarded areas, designed to distract and to weaken the defenses and/or balance

**Budo**: The path or way of martial arts.

**Dan ranks**: A black belt ranking such as Shodan, Nidan, Sandan, Yondan, etc. Dan means level.

**Deshi**: Student.

**Do**: Way or path. The third character in Aikido.

**Dojo**: A training hall for traditional Japanese arts, including Aikido and other martial arts. Do means way and jo means place.

**Gi**: Traditional uniform, usually white, worn during the practice of Japanese or Okinawan martial arts. Also known as a dogi or keiko gi.

**Gokyo**: Pinning throw with wrist/elbow lock; fifth technique

**Gyaku-hanmi**: Partners stand with opposite feet forward; for example, one with right foot forward and the other with left forward.

**Hai**: At its most basic, this term means "yes," but it also means okay; understood; I've got it; here/present; right; agreement; and acknowledgement that one is listening.

**Hajime**: Command to begin.

**Hakama**: A traditional Japanese outer garment worn over the gi pants. Black or blue in color, they are more formal, provide protection in rolling and falling and help conceal foot movement. Traditionally, they are worn by students holding the rank of Shodan and above.

**Hanmi**: A way of standing in Aikido so that the feet form a T-stance and the body is turned at an angle.

**Hanmi Handachi**: Techniques executed from a kneeling position against an attacker who is standing.

**Hiji Dori**: Elbow grab.

**Ikkyo**: Pinning throw; first technique.

**Irimi**: Entering; moving into and through the line of attack with no thought of escape.

**Irimi Nage**: Entering throw; many variations.

**Jiyu Waza**: Free style techniques or practice.

**Juji Nage**: Throw with Uke's arm crossed in a "t" in front of body.

**Kaiten Nage**: Rotational throw.

**Kata Menuchi**: Shoulder grab and strike.

**Kata Tori**: Shoulder grab.

**Katate Tori**: Single wrist grab.

**Keiko**: Training in traditional Japanese arts such as Aikido, flower arranging, or tea ceremony.

**Ki**: The vital force of the body. Through Aikido training, the ki of a person can be drawn in increasing amounts from the universe.

**Kiai**: A loud shout accompanying the execution of martial arts techniques.

**Kihon**: Basic techniques, as opposed to flowing techniques or variations.

**Kokyu Nage**: Breath throw; many variations.

**Koshi Nage**: Hip throw.

**Kote Gaeshi**: Wrist twist throw and pin.

**Kyu ranks**: The ranks before black belt (see Dan ranks), including Ikkyu, Nikyu, Sankyu, Yonkyu, Gokkyu, Rokkyu. Kyu ranks descend in order, with Ikkyu (1st kyu) being higher rank than Rokkyu (6th kyu). The opposite occurs in Dan ranks.

**Men-uchi / Shomen-uchi**: A straight strike to the head from the front with the hand or bokken.

**Morote Tori**: Grabbing the wrist with both hands.

**Mune Tsuki**: A straight punch or thrust to the center of the chest.

**Nage**: The partner who executes the technique; the partner throwing.

**Nikyo**: Pinning throw with wrist lock; second technique.

**Omedetou gozaimasu**: Congratulations!

**Omote**: The attacker's front; moving in front of your partner.

**One-gai Shimasu**: A phrase used to ask a favor of someone, in this case, "Will you please train with me?"

**O-Sensei**: Used to refer to the Founder of Aikido, Morihei Ueshiba (1883-1969). Literally, O means great and sensei means teacher.

**Randori**: A movement exercise used to develop calm and efficient blending with the power and movement of multiple attacks.

**Ryote Tori**: Grabbing both hands.

**Sankyo**: Pinning throw with wrist lock; third technique.

**Seiza**: A formal kneeling position. Also, the command to sit in seiza.

**Sempai**: Senior. In Japan, how one behaves toward others is dictated largely by one's status in terms of seniority, from martial arts dojos to schools and workplaces.

**Sensei**: In Japan, a title used to address or refer to a teacher. Literally, sei means born and sen means before.

**Shiho Nage**: Four-directional throw.

**Shikkou**: Knee walking.

**Shodan**: First degree black belt.

**Shomen**: The alcove at the front of the dojo, considered a sacred space, to which we pay respect in Aikido practice.

**Soto Deshi**: Students who do not live at the dojo. Soto means outside. See also Uchi Deshi.

**Suwari Waza**: Sitting (kneeling) techniques.

**Tachi**: Japanese sword.

**Tachi Dori**: Techniques of taking an opponent's sword and throwing him. Tachi means sword and dori means taking.

**Tachi Waza**: Standing techniques.

**Taijutsu**: Body techniques. The techniques of Aikido done without weapons.

**Tanto**: Wooden knife.

**Tanto Dori**: Knife-taking. Tanto means knife and dori means taking techniques.

**Tenchi Nage**: Heaven & Earth throw, with Nage's arms reaching up toward the sky and down to the ground.

**Tsuki**: A thrust or punch.

**Uchi**: A strike.

**Uchi Deshi**: Students who live at the dojo and train intensively. Uchi means inside. See also Soto Deshi.

**Uke**: The partner who is thrown or receives the technique (see also Nage.).

**Ukemi**: The art and skill of rolling and falling as a means of protecting the body from injury during the execution of Aikido techniques.

**Ura**: The attacker's back. Moving around or behind your partner. Opposite of Omote.

**Ushiro Ryote Tori**: Both wrists grabbed from the rear.

**Yame**: The command to stop.

**Yokomen**: Side of the head, strike to the side of the head.

**Yonkyo**: Pinning throw with pressure/nerve compression; fourth technique.

**Yudansha**: Persons holding rank of black belt (Shodan, Nidan, etc.).

# Photo Credits

Aikido of San Leandro
Sharon Fibelkorn (back cover)
Daniel Giberson
Charles Groff
Kei Izawa
Kent Krumveida
Kiryu Aikido dojo
Mary Mueller Rusin
Tanshinjuku dojo
Mark Waldron

Made in United States
Orlando, FL
12 June 2024

47810287R00134